Michelle Kirby

D1526729

Dedication

I dedicate this book to my wonderful husband, Tony and our four kids, Joshua, Arissa, TJ and Bri, who have always loved me unconditionally for who I am, and not for what I do. They have been so loving, graceful, and understanding—and even protective of me—while my journey to self-discovery unfolded and my quest for healing took place.

I also dedicate this book to you, the reader, and I hope that my story helps you to better understand that we are not defined by our pasts. We all make mistakes and bad choices, but that doesn't need to be the legacy we leave behind in this life. I can honestly say now, "Thank God, because there truly is a light at the end of the tunnel!" But through my healing journey, I have

3

also realized that the real responsibility lies *on us* to

"turn the light back on."

Michelle Kirby

Contents

Turn the *Light* Back On

Michelle Kirby

Foreword

Michelle Kirby is a brave human being who shares a life-transforming spiritual ordeal that could have wrecked her life and that of many others, especially her husband and children. The author is an intelligent, beautiful wife and mother, a successful entrepreneur, and an overtly happy go-getter who suddenly suffered a massive and transforming emotional and spiritual breakdown. Suddenly this lively young woman became numb and disinterested in life, inexplicably wallowing in pain and confusion, and complaining that God had abandoned her; however, the more she seemed to fight with God, the closer she felt Him in her heart and mind.

Turn the Light Back On is a powerful testimony of faith and redemption. This book is a

Turn the *Light* Back On

worthy gem grounded in biblical wisdom and

affirmations that shed light on complex

psychological traumas that likely originated in

negative early childhood experiences.

Dr. Genaro Marin

Professor of Psychology and Counseling

The City University of New York (Ret.)

Michelle Kirby

Introduction

This book was written purely to enhance the lives of the readers who find it in their hands. My goal is to paint the truest and most accurate picture of my life that I can, and in doing so, provide the hope for understanding, acceptance, and victory to anyone who identifies with or relates to any part of my life's story. My intention and hope is that this book would act as a conduit for me to share the lessons I have learned about life, and the wisdom I have gained as a result. This book's sole purpose is to empower you, the reader, to see that despite the many curveballs that life may throw at you, within your DNA lies the innate ability to get back up, dust yourself off, throw the ball back into the field, and to try again. As you read this story of my own life, it may seem unfortunate to you at times. Please know that I now look back at it all as a triumph! By faith *I made it!* By reading and studying God's Word, I overcame. I conquered life's battles—because God's Word told me that I am more than a conqueror! SO ARE YOU—AND YOU WILL CONQUER YOUR CIRCUMSTANCES, TOO!

Writing this book from a place of healing has allowed me to see things as they truly are. My full understanding, only achieved through having made it through all of my challenges, has allowed me now to provide important insights for your own life. Hopefully you can relate your own past pains to my own, and begin to see that you have the ability to overcome them yourself, and realize the fact that *they do not define your life!*

I am so humbled, as well as thankful, that the events that took place in my life did not prevent me from achieving anything my life was meant to offer. God is still using my life to minister to other to people—my real purpose. I truly believe that I had to go through all of these experiences in order to share my journey with others just like you. I hope my story blesses you. My prayer is that you will begin to find closure and healing for your life's greatest hurts. As you read, I hope that you identify with and can see parallels of my journey within your own life. And I pray that you find clarity, comfort, and the peace that transcends all understanding.

In talking with many people throughout my road to recovery, I now recognize that many of us do everything we can to mask the pain of our pasts: This a very common coping mechanism for human beings. I eventually realized that we take our unresolved feelings into adulthood, and when they are not dealt with they can pose a huge problem for us. This realization became a pivotal turning point for me. The only thing that gave me peace and allowed for my full healing was my faith. My faith allowed me to take the posture of knowing that God would deliver me from the darkness that gripped my life. It was my only glimmer of hope. And yet, even though it was seemingly microscopic in size, my "mustard seed" faith—or lack thereof—was the only thing I really needed.

Today, I have no regrets in my life because I truly understand and have come to know that our lives are not lived only for ourselves. All of our trials, obstacles, tough times, and tragedies are ultimately meant to bless others in some way, shape or form. I never looked at my past and wondered, *Why me?* Instead I look at my past and ask myself, *What am I really supposed to do with all this?*

Throughout this book, I will use short stories to share my life experiences and how I felt at the time when they occurred. Now, as an adult, I have learned that through the reading and studying of God's Word, we can find forgiveness, acceptance, and understanding. I have finally been able to come to a place of peace and healing—and I believe that you can, too. My healing process was not achieved overnight; in fact, it took me about two to three years to come to the place of full understanding. I had to first learn to let go of all the things in my past that had once gripped me. I had chosen to suppress them, dealing with them in silence. As you read my story, you will see that when I followed this path, things did not go very well for me.

So join me now as I describe the journey of my life and paint for you the picture of a woman who was once broken, hurt, ashamed, lonely, abused, and frightened. A woman who so often felt like a confused little girl who never was given the opportunity to grow up under "normal circumstances." Instead she had to fight her way through life as best she could. Although I now can see this as a victory—because I am now on the other side of it—certain events had me in denial for such a long time that I remained in bondage to my past. I learned to hide behind the shadows of my pain as a coping mechanism, not understanding that one day, many years later in my adult life, those shadows would consume me, along with the loved ones who were the closest to me.

In the summer of 2014, I hit the lowest and darkest moment in my life. I was admitted to a behavioral center hospital, and kept there for nine long days. I was experiencing frequent panic attacks, anxiety, insomnia, and a lack of appetite, having completely lost any zest for life. I had fallen into a deep, seemingly inescapable depression, and it seemed to me that coming out of it would be impossible for me to accomplish in my own strength. I was so gripped by fear, night terrors, and recurring nightmares from experiences in my past that I could no longer handle the pain. While there in the hospital, I decided to take an inventory of my life and try to discern where I was the most vulnerable. Honestly, I did not understand what was going on with me or what had caused the sudden negative change in how I was feeling and my approach to life.

At that time, it seemed that life as I knew it would never be the same again, and that was the most frightening feeling in the world. I felt as though there would be no possible way to ever be happy again, because the negativity that had consumed me seemed so permanent. There was just no end in sight. In this book, I will share with you, in full detail, this very difficult time in my life, because it was such a turning point for me. It was an eye-opening, yet beyond-scary experience that I wish no one else to ever experience for themselves!

From the outside looking in, to other people I really seemed to have it all together. How could this have happened to such a positive, happy-go-lucky woman? That is a very good question. I was a newlywed, recently married to the love of my life and with no worries in the world—until suddenly life as I knew it was turned upside down. And the most frightening part of all was that I actually *did* think that I "had it all together." I read every self-help book I could find that might help, and I even sought out counseling (although I was still claiming that "I'm okay!")

The purpose of my transparency here is to encourage you to seek help with your own struggles, to talk about how you are feeling and how those feelings are impacting your well-being. Begin to put your life into perspective as you process your pain, start to release it, and seek to forgive those who hurt you. I know that this can be a painful part of the process, but for your own quality of life, this is paramount.

When I truly came to realize what had occurred to me and why—after I hit my lowest point—I finally was able to put my life into perspective and truly understand my purpose in life. Now I live to empower people with my experiences. My hope is that I can help prevent others from having to go through what once consumed my life, because they never dealt with the pain of their own past. While speaking with many mentors, friends, and acquaintances, I learned that they too, have hit rock bottom at some point in their lives because they suppressed their pain rather than deal with it. I am here to shed light on what can happen to us if we don't properly process the pain in our past experiences, and the best way for me to achieve this is to fully disclose the events that took place in my own life—the circumstances that led me to that hospital room, my own "rock bottom."

I must warn you, this series of events I will be sharing is not for the "faint at heart". During my years of healing, I was consumed with reading and studying the Scriptures, especially passages that spoke God's healing to my pain. At the end of each chapter of this book, I will share the "life verse(s)" I discovered that literally helped me take my life back and move forward into the future God had for me. I will share my own insights on these verses, as well as give you time and space to reflect on your personal journey to healing. In this way, you too can follow God's path toward healing and understanding in your own life. And at the end of each part of my story, I have provided a place for your personal reflections. These can help you to highlight those pivotal points in your own life that may have adversely impacted you, and help you identify ways you can move past the pain.

And finally, I would ask that you take an honest emotional inventory of your own heart, to be sure that you are not unnecessarily holding on to any hurts from the past. Use this book as a tool: Write notes in the margins, highlight anything that stands out to you, mark it up and make it your own, and then share it with others to help them, as well. Allow my story to help you to see that your life *does* have a purpose and that you are *not* a product of your past! You and me—we

are fighters, and we are winners!

1

The Beginning of Denial

My mom was very young when she gave birth to me; in fact, she became pregnant with me at the age of fifteen. She really wasn't in a good place in her life to become a mom. She couldn't know how to be a mother since she was still a child herself.

My mother was very abusive to me when I was a child, and I grew to become very frightened of her. As I grew up, I tried to justify the beatings she continually rained upon me. I would make excuses for her in a vain attempt to make my own self feel better. Many nights I fell asleep with tears streaming down my face, crying in silence from the fear of her hearing me and beating me yet again. In this way, bottling up emotions became "my thing"—my typical coping mechanism—and I was determined to master it for the sake of my survival.

I was born in the Bronx, in New York City, in the early seventies, and for the most part the things I know about the time between my birth and when I turned six years old are from the stories my family members have shared with me. We moved around a lot, there never seemed to be any stability. The places we lived in ranged from an apartment building in the Bronx with my father, to the Dominican Republic, where we lived for just a month when I was about a year old. When we returned to New York, the apartment building in which we had been living was no longer in a habitable living condition. There was no running water and no heat, so my mom decided to take us to my father's mother's house to live. Despite being my "grandma," I was told that she wanted nothing to do with me and that she wouldn't even hold me when I was a baby.

With my mom having had me at such a young age, I can only imagine how much of a burden I was to her. I never really knew my father, and I have no childhood memories of him, although I did meet him when I was older, in my late twenties. Still, my mom could have easily chosen to have had an abortion or she could have put me up for adoption—but then I wouldn't be where I am today and my life would look much different. From stories I've been told, my father wouldn't buy groceries for my mother and me; he would just sit around drinking beer, hoping a job would simply come to him. Because my mom didn't have any money, she had no bed, and so she used to sleep on the floor while I slept in a crib. She would actually sneak into my grandmother's house and "steal" food in order to create baby food for me from what she could find. When my grandmother moved into the Baychester Projects, I was about two years old, and at that time she allowed my mom and me to stay there with her. It was a full house at that point, but it was fun for the most part, or so I have been told.

When I was four years old, we moved to Tampa, Florida, and my aunt and godmother went along to help my mom to care for me. I do have a few memories of our time in Tampa, where we lived for about two and a half years. I can remember a lot of the animals: Our neighbors had chickens, I got a rabbit one Easter, and we had a Yorkshire terrier for a while that ran away one day and broke my heart.

Shortly after that time, my aunt took me back to live with her at my grandparents' house until my mom could come join us. I was about six years old at that point. Life at my grandma's house at that time holds some of my fondest childhood memories. After never having felt true love from my mom, I was suddenly surrounded by family members, and their presence masked my feelings of loneliness and being unwanted.

I didn't see my mother much during this time because when she was home, she was sleeping because she worked nights. She had to work three jobs to make ends meet at that time. I was the first grandchild in the family, so everyone spoiled me, not with material things, but with love. I can remember watching my grandfather "bless the house" as he did every Sunday: He played "hallelujah music" (as I called it) and he'd burn incense while walking through the house praying. I still can remember the sweet aroma that would fill the house as he did that. This began my exposure to what it looked like to worship God.

Living in my grandparents' home there in Baychester, I experienced a few funny incidents, coupled with several awkward moments.

The first funny memory I have from that time was the trouble that my love for chocolate would get me into. I would see my grandparents oftentimes eating some "chocolate" out of a small blue carton. It seemed strange to me that they would go to the bathroom and take it out of the medicine cabinet to eat it, but I thought that they must have been hiding it from me because they knew how much I loved chocolate and candy. I decided that I would "show them," and so I snuck into the bathroom one day to eat it all! I sat on the toilet cover, locked the door, and then mischievously opened the blue container of Ex-Lax and ate it like nobody's business. I do remember leaving one piece intact, because I didn't want the entire box to seem empty. Little did I know that I'd be spending almost an entire day on the toilet getting rid of what I'd eaten—and much more! It was so awful. I felt like I was in the movie *Dumb and Dumber*, in the part where Jim Carrey poured a constipation elixir into his buddy's tea. Are you picturing the scene? Well, that was me—but as a pitiful little girl who only wanted to eat chocolate.

Another funny incident I recall (which was only "funny" until I got busted and was in big trouble) took place when one day I was skating around the house, repeating the words "*El diablo, el diablo*," which in English means "the devil." Apparently, I wasn't supposed to say that word; it was like a curse word in my grandparents' home, and I found myself with a stick of soap in my mouth when it was time for me to take my bath.

My feelings were hurt, since it was my grandma
who made me eat the soap. To this day I'm not a
fan of ivory soap!

I can't remember much more in any detail
from when I was so young, but several things
really stood out: I knew I was loved by my
grandma; my aunt did most of the cooking for
me; my mom worked far too much; and my
uncles had a "marijuana tree" in their room.
Besides these more innocent memories, the one
incident that left an indelible mark upon my mind
and spirit was that when I was six years old, one
of my uncles fondled me in the bathroom. From
that moment on, I felt completely helpless,
confused, and uncomfortable around him—and
every other man, for that matter.

Needless to say, that never happened
again, and for that I am thankful. I forgive him
now, but I know that this was the origin of my

distrust in men. My guess is that he was just a curious, "horny" young man who was trying to explore his sexuality with a young niece—and obviously this is not an uncommon thing in our world unfortunately.

My AHA Moment:

Not much happened during this time in my life that left any lasting impressions on me, other than the situation with my uncle. I have never shared that experience until the writing of this book. For many years afterward, I felt ashamed, embarrassed, dirty, and frightened, and I know now that I was in denial this had ever happened to me for many years.

In your own life, please remember that situations that occurred *to you* do not *define who you are*. Frequently, once you realize the motives of the person who hurt you or the reasons behind the situation, you can understand that you simply

might have been at the wrong place at the wrong

time. With that understanding, it becomes easier

to shed light on "what really happened," and then

let it go and move on. When most of us

remember our childhood, we often gravitate

toward the moments that make us feel happy, that

remind us of fun times and the love we

experienced—and we tend to suppress the

negative experiences, because, after all, we were

"just kids" trying to enjoy our childhood. We

must recognize that we are not alone. Many of us

have experienced things in childhood that we may

have never even talked about to anyone yet.

Your AHA moment:

Are there any moments from your early

childhood you might have suppressed that still

manage to find their way into your thoughts

today? If so, write them down here and let's begin

your journey to healing!

_____

_____

_____

The LORD is close to the brokenhearted and saves those

who are crushed in spirit.

Psalm 34:18 NIV

This verse is so powerful! It made me realize that

I had never been forsaken by God, and that He

was still there with me even when I was crushed,

down, and out, when I felt as if I didn't have

anyone else in this world on my side. I held on to

this verse throughout my healing process, and it

helped to bring me so much comfort.

2

Little Girls Left to Cope

My younger sister was born when I was seven years old and my mom and I were living with her father, my stepdad. I was so excited that I now had a sibling to share my life with. I fell in love with my baby sister from the moment I laid my eyes on her. She became the love of my life. I felt so much safer with her around, thinking that perhaps my mom would beat me less often because she wouldn't want my sister to witness her behaving like that.

Well, I was wrong. Not only was I still constantly getting beaten by my mom, but my mother and stepfather would also fight and scream, even go after each other with knives.

They would fight like two grown men; I could hardly believe my eyes at times at what they did. I saw them punching each other in the face, and I can still remember the sounds of the slaps, punches, and shoves against the walls and closet doors. I remember thinking one day that instead of just cleaning his gun (my stepdad was a corrections officer at Rikers Island), he would turn and use it on her, because their fights were so intense, both verbally and physically.

Little girls should never have to live in that kind of environment, let alone grow used to it. It was uncommon for my sister and me to ever experience a night of peace (unless I was spending the night with my aunt or my sister's aunt from her dad's side). At that time, there wasn't any consistent sense of peace in my life at all. I can't say I ever got used to the chaos in our home, because no little girl gets used to seeing her mom being beaten by someone who supposedly loved her, and then in turn receive her own beating. Life in our household soon turned into a vicious cycle, because the more she was beaten, the more she beat me. I couldn't win for trying.

I can remember trying to hide my little sister in the closet of our bedroom and cover her ears. It was a terrible experience. It eventually became so extreme that my little sister was taken out of the situation and sent to Puerto Rico when she was about two years old. After that, I was so scared, lonely, and confused. I resented the fact that it was considered so "unhealthy" for her to live in such a violent atmosphere, but apparently the situation was acceptable for me. Where was my rescuer? Was I not good enough to be saved?

At this point in my childhood, I can honestly remember hating my life. I hated my mother for fighting so violently with my stepdad and for sending my little sister away. I hated the fact that I had essentially been left alone in my terrible situation. When my sister finally did come back, I was happy, but before that time I had missed her so much, it was devastating. As a child, I had no idea what was going on or whether my sister would ever return to our family. I would look at pictures of her wearing diapers and running along the beach, and all I could think was, *Will I ever see my sister again?* The beatings by my mother continued; getting hit almost every day, and it was quickly becoming too much to bear. Hatred was filling my heart—I could almost feel the stones beginning to form and my heart tightening up as a result of the environment in which I was being raised.

My AHA moment:

My childhood at this point seemed to be filled with many violent, scary moments; all I can really recall was the constant feeling of a large pit in my stomach, and it never went away. I hated my life, and I hated my mother. When I finally decided, later in my life, to remove the hatred and resentment from my heart, true forgiveness became possible. This also helped to open the door for my own healing to begin and for healthier relationships to be formed with maternal females whom God would bring into my life. I began to realize that I wasn't defined by the abuse and the violence that had surrounded me, but that this was a choice that others had made about how they treated me. I made the decision to forgive my mom, because, deep down inside myself, I had always thought that she must have been traumatized herself at some point, to have caused her to put her hands on me with such force and frequency.

Your AHA moment:

Were you ever abused as a child by a loved one?
Do you still hold resentment and unforgiveness in
your heart toward that person? Or were you
raised in such a violent environment that it
shaped how you view your relationships today? I
would challenge you now to pray for the courage
to identify, to forgive, and to release your hatred
and pain so that you can truly move past it. If
there is someone in your life who hurt you and
they are actually willing to talk about what
happened, perhaps that would bring the closure
you need to move on and forgive them fully.

On these lines, list the persons who
abused you in the past, and any steps God brings
to your mind that would help you to forgive
them.

Michelle Kirby

_____

_____

_____

Do not judge, and you will not be judged. Do not condemn, and you will not be condemned. Forgive, and you will be forgiven.

Luke 6:37 NIV

This verse always reminds me that each of us will someday come before the Lord for judgment, to account for all of our wrongdoings. How could I confess my own sins, ask God for forgiveness, and be restored to a right standing with Him, and yet not forgive my mom? That would be going against the principles I learned from God's Word, and so the decision to forgive my mother was made with no regrets and from a sincere heart.

3

Just Say NO!

The large pit in my stomach, which I had become so accustomed to as a child, was directly related to the environment and conditions in which I had been living. My mom didn't know how to be a mother to me, and I felt like I was always a burden to her. She was just a kid herself when she gave birth to me. It eventually became so bad for me that many of my babysitters, my aunts and neighbors would tell me they were going to call the cops or social services on my mom, but nothing ever came of it. Everyone would tell her to stop hitting me, and my aunts even threatened to take me away from her, but still nothing changed. My life just degenerated into a mere existence, in which getting hit, slapped, beaten with any object she could find (including a belt or an extension cord), or even being made to kneel on raw rice pellets for long periods of time as a form of punishment. I grew accustomed to being her personal release for all of the aggressions she felt as a result of the life that she herself had created for herself. I did not want to live with my mom anymore, since I felt like I had become her personal punching bag. I was just a child, but I was hit all the time—and most of the time I had done nothing wrong! It was such a horrible existence for me; I literally lived a great portion of my childhood in fear, despair, and loneliness, and the emotional damage this inflicted on me left me virtually devastated.

You see, my top "love languages" are physical touch and words of affirmation, but when a person is being physically abused, especially by his or her mom, a lasting mark is left upon that person's soul. Such a wound is very hard to recover from—but, as you can see from my life, it's not impossible.

As I mentioned before, I did not want to live at home with my mom, and so I would find any and every excuse to sleep over at other people's houses. I stayed at my aunt's house on most weekends—she lived on Crescent Avenue in the Bronx at that time, and I knew this became an issue between my mom and her sister. More and more resentment and tension was in the air. The love I should have had for my mother was growing stronger for my aunt instead, and this brought a lot of problems for me and my mom in the future. It led to us growing further apart and not ever really cultivating a relationship. To make matters worse, on one occasion the aunt who had been chosen to be my godmother asked me to sleep over at her house because she saw I was favoring my other aunt and she wanted me to spend more time with her. Little did she know that I was not fond of her husband, so I tried not to sleep over at her place. Her husband seemed to behave inappropriately toward me at times; he would look at my mom in inappropriate ways, as well, and his flirting rubbed me the wrong way. I didn't trust him, and it seemed like he was up to no good.

On one particular weekend, to appease my godmother, I took her up on her offer to spend the weekend with her. Because she was also my aunt, it only seemed fair that I would spend some time with her, too. However, the final night of that weekend was also the last time I'd ever stay over at her place.

I was watching TV that evening when her husband came into the living room and sat down on the edge of the sofa bed where I had been laying. He picked up the remote control and changed the TV to a pornographic channel. That was the first time I'd ever seen such a thing in my life. Both the visual images and the noises the people were making terrified me—and all the while, I was wondering, *Where is my godmother?* Apparently her husband had seen that she had just jumped in the shower, which always took her a very long time.

After a few minutes of watching the pornography on the television, this grown man asked me to show him my private parts, and told me that in turn he would show me his own. I had the immediate good judgment to jump up and run in search of my godmother, which was how I learned that she was, indeed, taking a shower. I pounded on the bathroom door and called to her that I needed to come in, but the door was locked. I sank down to the floor just outside the bathroom door, shaking with rage that he would dare to ask me to do such a thing. I sat there with the taste of my own tears as they ran down my face, waiting for her to get out of the shower and open the door.

To this day, my godmother really doesn't understand exactly what took place. After I left the room, her husband actually panicked, ran into a different room, and shut the door—and he never approached me again. At that time I had begun to wonder whether all men were going to be total letdowns. As I mentioned earlier, I don't have any memory of my dad, and one of my uncles hadn't left me with a warm fuzzy feeling. My mom consistently dated "weirdos," and then my godmother's husband had asked to see me naked? Why? What were his intentions with me? I was only eight years old!

Now that I am an adult, I believe that he was not in his right mind. He later went on to take a gun and shoot it all throughout the same room he ran into that night. He later claimed he was "going crazy" so that he could get disability pay from the government and not have to keep a job. When I consider just what I have told you about so far, I'm so thankful now for the things that I have overcome in my life. But as you read on, you will realize just how broken I became, and how my life took many strange turns—for the worse.

My AHA Moment:

I spent many of my childhood years getting beaten so frequently and violently—sometimes for no apparent reason. For so many years I was literally terrified of my mom. I was just a kid, and I needed to be loved and nurtured, to feel wanted—and not by anyone other than my mom. I fully forgive her now, because I understand that no one hurts their children because they want to. Something deeply rooted in them has pushed them to the point that they no longer care about anyone or anything around them. When I think of my mother that way, I feel such compassion for all that she might have been subjected to. They must have been terrible to have made her take her rage out on me like such a monster. As for my own life, experiencing a rough childhood or even difficulties later in life doesn't truly justify what she did to me—because I did not go on to beat my own kids—but we all have our own ways of dealing with the challenges in our lives and we all make decisions that we, in turn, have to live with. I can't say that my relationship with my mom has been fully restored, but I do love her and I have fully and sincerely forgiven her for the way she treated me when I was growing up.

As for my godmother's husband, back then he just added to the fear of men that I already had, but fortunately I never had to deal with him again. At the time, it was frightening, but now I know that I was actually spared a possibly worse outcome. I knew deep inside that I had the upper hand in the situation and the right to stand up for myself and "just say no."

Your AHA Moment:

Were any relationships that you experienced when you were growing up "inappropriate" in any way? Do you have any resentment toward someone who, instead of loving and caring for you, hurt you so badly that you are still angry at them? Take the time to write down anything that comes to mind now, anything you might have suppressed or have purposely chosen not to think about so you wouldn't feel the pain of the experience. Now write it down, forgive the person, and begin to let it all go.

_____

_____

_____

_____

Bear with each other and forgive one another if any of you has a grievance against someone. Forgive as the Lord forgave you.

Colossians 3:13 NIV

During my time of healing, when I would break down sobbing, I would repeat this verse to myself over and over. It helped me to forgive my mom and many others who hurt me and stole my childhood. I was continually reminded that we *all* have to account for our wrongdoings before the

Michelle Kirby

Lord. I cannot judge my mom—or anyone else for that matter. In forgiving them, I should not even be concerned with whether or not they have truly "repented." I have to check my own heart to be sure that I have genuinely forgiven them so that the Lord will have mercy on me for my own indiscretions.

4

Do *All* Men Suck?

After my stepdad left my mom, a series of different "boyfriends" coming over to our house began. My mom would cut hair on the side to make money, and from the outside looking in, it seems that she dated every one of her male clients. I'm not completely sure that is true, but it certainly felt like that was what was going on. I did not like most of the men who came over to our house, and one guy in particular gave me the "heebie-jeebies." He was young—he seemed too young to be involved with my mom—and he had very short hair, which didn't seem to need that much cutting or styling. But he would still come over often, and to me he had the worst Adam's apple I had ever seen. My sister and I were sometimes sent to bed early, and then we were subjected to noises a child should never have to hear. I would take my little sister to our room and put her to bed, then go into the closet to cry and pray myself to sleep. Seeing my mom being so affectionate with men irritated me. It made me wonder how she could have love enough for them but never enough for me.

I went through my elementary- and middle-school years suffering physical and verbal abuse from her, but I also seemed to end up in classes with unkind female teachers—and one male teacher who actually threw a chair at his students when he lost his temper in the classroom! *Do all men suck?* I seriously began to wonder.

When I finally changed schools to start the seventh grade, I finally had a teacher I liked—

a cool, handsome, and charismatic male teacher. I'm not going to lie: I was on cloud nine! That school year turned out to be awesome, filled with fun field trips and lots of positive attention and accolades for my good grades. Meeting my teacher's two sons—who were both absolutely adorable; the girls all fought for their attention—was the icing on the cake for me. Somehow my luck seemed to be changing in life. I not only was the "teacher's pet," but his sons loved me, as well, and they always showed it. We would all go out to eat at lunch, hang out with the other kids, and joke around. It was so much fun—until I came up with the brilliant idea to introduce this handsome teacher to my mom so they could date.

I don't know if I wanted this to happen more for her, so she could settle down with someone nice, or for me, since I so enjoyed the innocent attention I was receiving from my teacher. Honestly, it was likely a combination of the two. I was only fourteen at the time, so he was definitely too old for me. But I still wanted him in my life, so maybe, just maybe, I thought, it could work out with him and my mom, and we could all live happily ever after together. Later on in my story, I will elaborate on my relationship with that teacher in more detail.

My AHA Moment:

When I was so young and saw all the men coming in and out of my mom's life, it was frightening for me. I didn't know whether they would try to hurt me, touch me, or just ask me weird or awkward questions. I also never knew when an argument would turn violent, because I knew that it could at any given moment. I now understand that watching my mother be affectionate with all of these men while she treated me so badly, would naturally leave me feeling resentful toward her. I would find peace during that time by running to my room and praying in my closet. It was the only comfort I knew. Now, looking back, I also understand that my mom was just looking for love and trying to feel desired and cared for herself. She was compensating for having never felt genuine love from a man, and she was looking for love from anyone who would pay attention to her. When one man didn't work out, she'd just try again with someone else. This chaotic home situation was what prompted me to play matchmaker; I was hoping that a good relationship would work out for her, and if she was happy with a man, then maybe she would love me more and hit me less.

Your AHA Moment:

Did you have someone close to you, during your childhood withhold love from you while they were affectionate with other people? Perhaps, like

me, you experienced uncertainty in your home or

family situation when you were growing up. Did

you ever find yourself nervous as you carried

adult burdens for a younger sibling? If any of

these thoughts resonate with you, jot down what

comes to mind. This will help you experience

closure and find peace with what actually

occurred, and then let go of your negative

feelings.

_____

_____

_____

_____

Even though I walk through the darkest valley, I will fear

no evil, for you are with me; your rod and your staff, they

comfort me.

Psalm 23:4 NIV

During my healing process, this verse helped me put so many things in my past into perspective. So often I felt alone and afraid, but I wasn't; God was always with me, and even as a child I knew I had a heavenly Father who would protect me and save me from messes before it was too late. This verse was very comforting, helping me to understand that even in my dark moments, He was ever-present with me.

5

The Awkward High School Years

Growing up without a father or a stable father figure, along with a mother who seemed to carry her life burdens so heavily, didn't create a good combination, at least not for me. I don't recall any interactions or times during my childhood or teenage years when I ever felt comfort or love from my mom. I did experience love from my grandma. (As I'm writing these words, I am actually on a plane, on my way to make arrangements for her funeral; she passed away on Tuesday, May 24, 2017. I'm so thankful I got to spend time with her in 2016.)

I had an awkward time feeling comfortable when I was in high school, but a lot of this was due to my attending three different high schools. My mom moved us around a lot. I tried to immerse myself in sports, because I wanted to stay out of trouble and also keep from being picked on. I was very skinny at the time, and I had low self-esteem and abandonment issues. There was no love in my home, and so everywhere else I went, I felt like an outcast.

So, when I was sixteen years old, I ran away from home. I could no longer take the beatings, the late-night crying spells, and my mom's erratic behavior. I no longer wanted to feel like a burden to her or have to listen to my sister cry whenever I was hit or yelled at. My mom had told me many times that if I didn't like her rules or agree with them, I could make the choice to leave. *Well, don't threaten me with a good time!* I thought. The idea of running away was frightening and exciting to me at the same time. When I left my house, I did so through my bedroom window. A guy who had a crush on me, whom I knew through his sister, came to my rescue and helped me with some of my belongings. At that point in my life, the fear I was experiencing was masked by the thought of the freedom that awaited me. I was the queen of denial, the master suppressor of hurts, but little did I know that the events and choices I would make from that point forward would put me in some very challenging situations.

The guy who helped me run away from home became my "boyfriend." We were apparently "dating," even though we had never said out loud that we were—and I didn't feel any love at all for him. I liked him as a friend, but it wasn't the "mushy" kind of "like." Before I spent

time with him, I hadn't been into dating. I was a
self-proclaimed "tomboy," only into sports
throughout high school. Unfortunately, I had lost
my virginity at age sixteen—with a jock from my
high school—and it was a horrible experience! I
remember feeling so much pain and wondering,
*What am I doing? This really hurts and I don't even love
this guy!* I now know that the reason I had sex with
this guy was to feel loved and to receive some
validation from someone—anyone—at that point,
because my home life was so turbulent.

In any case, moving in with this new
"boyfriend" felt scary to me, because the only
men I had come across at this point in my life had
let me down. To me, he was the only way out, but
no one really helps anyone for free—at least this
was not the case for me at this time.

I lived with this guy for about a month,
but he started wanting a lot of things from me

that I wasn't comfortable giving up to him so freely. He was nice, but I just "wasn't feeling it." I kept recalling the things from my past, and, honestly, I just wanted to be loved, cared for, and taken care of with no expectations from me and no more pain. I just wanted my mental pain to stop once and for all. I had no point of reference of love from a man, nor had I seen it mirrored in the relationships I had seen in my home. All I could think was, *I don't want to be treated the way I heard my mom being treated in the bedroom when I was younger.* This time of disgust and fear caused me to start searching for better options of where to stay. I found myself jumping around a bit until I finally had the brightest of ideas. Are you ready for this? Remember I mentioned earlier that we would be revisiting the teacher? Yes, the charismatic, handsome teacher who dated my mother for a brief period of time. *Well*, I thought, *why not reach out to him?* He had shown me so much love and respect before, and he would probably perfectly understand my pain and struggles, and the history I had with my mom. When I contacted him, he told me that he had stopped dating my mom because he "didn't date her for her"—whatever that meant. He further went on to tell me that he had wanted to "keep tabs on me" and that he hadn't agreed with how she had treated me.

My search for love and freedom came with a price. There were consequences to my actions that later led to some unfortunate circumstances in my life. The choices I was to make and the life in which I was to become immersed at that point would soon take turn after turn for the worse.

My AHA Moment:

At this point in my life, I was so fed up with everything that had happened to me. I was more than ready to just live my life alone, to make my own decisions and get out of my mom's house. I did resent being forced to grow up so quickly, but the reality was, I wasn't mature enough at that time to deal with what life would throw at me, but I believed that I could make the best of it somehow or that I would suffer trying. I was determined to find comfort, happiness, and some glimmer of hope after the chaotic sixteen years I had lived so far. I was angry at my mom; I felt that I had been really given no choice and that I had been pretty much forced out of our home. Nothing I did ever pleased her. I made A's in school, and I also held down a part-time job, but she would still fight with me for buying too many shoes (with my own money). I resented her because I had dropped out of high school during my senior year, because I was afraid she'd find me at my school. Instead, I got my GED, passing with flying colors. My teachers were so disappointed that I missed out on prom and graduation, and that I had forfeited all my awards, my accolades, and my shot at being the class valedictorian.

Now, in retrospect, I realize that as humans, we are meant to survive anything that is placed in front of us; we are resilient, strong individuals who can overcome anything in our paths—everything besides death! I also realize that this pivotal point in my life would become a defining moment. At the time, I was just trying to find myself and find out who I really was. But from a very young age, I knew and felt that God had so many greater things in store for my life.

Your AHA Moment:

Have you ever done something so spontaneous—like running away?—that you felt you had well thought out and knew exactly what steps to take?

But did you later discover that the results of your action wasn't everything that you had pictured it would be? Have you ever found yourself making decisions that you later realize had compromised the integrity you had tried so hard to maintain? This is normal; we all go through these types of things. Take some time to really think through the answers to these questions, and make sure you don't have any regrets or suppressed feelings that are affecting your current relationships in a negative way. Write these down, pray over them, release them, and let them all go.

_____

_____

_____

For I know the plans I have for you, declares the LORD, plans to prosper you and not to harm you, plans to give you hope and a future.

Jeremiah 29:11 NIV

This verse helped me to find real closure with my past. I had known all along that God had great plans for me; this was evident through my academic grades and athletic achievements. I knew that one day I would live out this purpose, but that it could take a while to figure out how that would happen. This has become one of my "life verses," and it helps me to this day to realize that when I am feeling discouraged or that my life is going in circles, if I seek Him He will reveal His plans to me and show me the way I should go.

Michelle Kirby

6

Too Good to Be True?

Before I start telling you about this part of my life, allow me to take you back to my junior high school days for a bit, back to when I met the charismatic teacher and his two sons. All the girls loved this teacher—including me. He was older and handsome, and he dressed so nicely and smelled so good. What was there not to like? I realize now that I probably was just reacting to seeing a "nice man" for the first time in my life. I had had crushes on many TV personalities, and I even wanted to marry the star of the show *CHIPS*— Eric Estrada. This seventh-grade teacher reminded me of that TV actor. He was very popular, as were his two sons, who visited the school often. All of them paid so much attention

71

to me, far above all of the other girls. They treated me so well that it blew my mind. I remember thinking, *Is this what it feels like to be loved, respected, wanted, and appreciated?* I finally felt good in my own skin when I was at school at that time.

As I had expected, my former teacher was more than thrilled to have me stay with them, and so I did for several years. At the beginning, I will admit that it was awesome. I was living with a man who seemed to worship the ground I walked on, and I was loving my life. Other girls would come and go in each of their lives, but I was the constant one who was allowed to stay with their family and share their lives. He did have a girlfriend, who I thought had a big head and too many teeth, but that was just me. Part of me was jealous, but more so it was because she seemed to be taking away some of the attention I wanted my former teacher to pay to me. The only time I felt good being around her was when I knew that she had to leave and that I would still be staying in the home. Needless to say, his relationship with her didn't last long, and I'm pretty sure that I might have had something to do with that. In my very young, naïve mind, my crush had transformed into love, and I felt that I would be a better girlfriend. I had decided that I would not allow him to show interest in anyone else, or keep her around, and so she was out of the picture very quickly.

The teacher insisted that I earn my stay, and so for the most part I turned over to him the paychecks from each of the many jobs that I tried to keep. My work life as a young adult consisted of jobs at fast-food restaurants and department stores. But as my relationship progressed with this man, I quickly learned how to feel and act like a "woman."

At that time, there was nothing I wouldn't do for this man and his boys. I remember thinking how happy I was that my luck seemed to be changing. But then, one summer my teacher ran into an old friend who was a cocaine dealer, and he became a frequent client that summer. I'm sure you can see where this is going. During the summer, when he was off of work, I first tried cocaine with him on the weekends when I didn't have to work. Our drug use went from experimental, to occasional, to almost daily usage—and that was when the "jumping around" between jobs came into play for me. I just couldn't hold down a solid job with my new cocaine habit. I found myself locked into a vicious cycle of confusion, as I experienced moments of bliss, euphoria, fear, paranoia, empowerment, and eventually deep regret.

I was soon initiating the phone calls for drugs and I would even go downstairs to make the purchase. The idea of doing something so scary, yet glorified by movies and TV, seemed exhilarating to me—until I noticed how it was changing my perception of life as well as my standards and integrity.

While under the influence of cocaine, I made many bad choices that landed me in trouble, much more trouble than I had bargained for. I did several things that I am not at all proud of, but I did them purely because I never had any money of my own; I had to give it all to the teacher.

I stole money from a fast-food restaurant where I worked by partially ringing up the orders and manipulating the system. How I didn't get caught at this is now a mystery to me. I also returned to my mom's house to retrieve some of my things, but not only did I walk out with my clothes, but I also took some of her jewelry and some money I found in one of her blazers. To me at that time, that was the equivalent of hitting the lottery jackpot! I considered myself justified in taking her jewelry and money because of all the beatings I had endured as a child.

After I made my way back to the condo where we were staying, my former teacher benefited more than me from that money. He insisted we go shopping for food, and I can remember our shopping as if we were preparing for a zombie apocalypse or something equally dramatic. We had about three shopping carts full of food.

I had been hoping to save money and not blow it all like that, in the hopes of leaving that situation someday soon. I didn't like the person I was becoming, and I had a gut feeling that things would only get worse for me if I stayed.

Michelle Kirby

My decisions and life choices were not getting any better. The downward spiral continued when we decided it would be a good idea for me to pass on some unpaid items at a cash register of a well-known department store where I worked. I'll never forget the terrible feeling I had when I was busted. When the authorities walked up to my register, took me away in handcuffs, and escorted me to the police patrol car waiting outside, I was in complete shock. To say I have some horror stories about my time in jail would be a lie; even though I was scared, I was greeted by some lesbians in the holding cell who thought I was so cute and they actually offered me some food to eat. I was only there overnight before the teacher bailed me out. The store miraculously dropped the charges against me, and my record was wiped clean.

At that point, though, I started to feel very used, and I no longer felt comfortable with this former teacher or his two sons. My gut instinct proved to be correct. When I saw things I didn't agree with and began to express my opinion to him more often, the dynamic of our relationship changed very quickly.

The next events of my life are more like living nightmares to me. I don't recall when the physical and verbal abuse started, but I will tell you that amidst all the smooth talk, subtle bribes, financial manipulation, brainwashing, and many other red flags I chose to ignore, this one caught me totally off guard. Allow me to explain.

As I mentioned earlier, I had felt like I was living the good life. All of my "superficial" needs were being met like never before; my ego, emotions, and pride were continually being stroked. I was told I was beautiful every single day, and I was given many ongoing compliments. Once I got a taste for this kind of life, I chose to forget how my own mother had once dated this man; to me, that was irrelevant. In my own mind, I was doing everything at that time for the love I had never had before, and for the attention and acceptance this man was offering to me. Despite our cocaine use and the dishonest things I was doing, I was still happy, excited, and loving life. I felt respected and accepted and loved. I stood with this man as long as I did because it seemed to be a safe place for me. But as you will soon see, all of the positive attention I had been receiving would not last.

My AHA Moment:

This time of my life was loaded with many emotions—both good and bad. The decisions I made, of leaving my mom's house, dropping out of school with only a few months left before graduation, searching desperately for a place to live, and compromising my morals and character as a result, had left me feeling empty. I was trying so hard to feel loved and accepted, but the choices I made to experiment with cocaine and to steal from my mom and my workplaces demonstrated my immaturity, my wrongdoing, and how I was living in survival mode. I truly didn't know what I was doing. I was highly influenced by the environment in which I was living, by the man I had chosen to live with, and most of the time I felt extremely trapped.

Denial and the suppression of my emotions were at a very high level at this time of my life, because I had convinced myself that I was happy and living the good life, when in fact I was actually in bondage to sex, drugs, theft, and lies. None of those things can make anyone feel whole, only emptier than ever before. In this particular chapter of my life, I had to heal and concentrate on self-forgiveness. I should have never broken into my mom's house and taken her money or jewelry. Those things didn't belong to me and there was no excuse for me to hide behind. Each time I did something that wasn't "good," I still felt a gentle presence hovering over my life, protecting me in the moments when I was the most weak and, honestly, acting quite stupid!

Your AHA Moment:

Is there anything you have done in the past that was so horrible that you had to go down on your knees and cry out for forgiveness? Maybe you haven't yet come to that moment of release or confession, because you have buried things so deep down in your mind that you don't even think about them anymore. God is such a gentle God, and He loves you right where you are in life.

Reflect on anything you might not have confessed to Him yet and then do so, so that you can experience His forgiveness and truly begin to walk in a right relationship with Him. Write these things down without shame, and begin to confess them out loud.

_____

_____

_____

Jesus said, "Father, forgive them, for they do not know what they are doing."

Luke 23:34 NIV

"And forgive us our debts as we also have forgiven our debtors."

Matthew 6:12 NIV

Repent, then, and turn to God, so that your sins may be wiped out, that times of refreshing may come from the Lord, and that He may send the Messiah, who has been appointed for you- even Jesus.

Acts 3:19–20 NIV

These verses were the primary scriptures I internalized during my healing process, because not only was I healing from past hurts, but I was also in denial of some of the things that I myself had done. Releasing these things and giving them to God, then confessing and surrendering my ways, allowed healing and self-forgiveness to fully take place and enter my heart and soul.

Michelle Kirby

7

And Now It Really Gets Ugly

One specific moment stands out to me as defining the route my life would begin to take. It was one of the most hurtful moments of my stay with them, and it opened my eyes to the type of people they were. And that was the beginning of the onset of violence toward me.

The moment I knew that things would forever change for me took place when we received the news in the mail that we were not able to have pets in our condo. We had already acquired the most beautiful pit bull puppy. He was perfect, and he was all I looked forward to getting home to see. But one day, we all got in the car and began to drive down a long winding road

85

that I wasn't familiar with. All of a sudden, the door flew open and my former teacher simply tossed our puppy right out of the car. *What!!!??* I thought. *Who does that?* The shock in my system immediately moved my mind into a replay of the past hurts in my life, and all of the feelings of terror, fear, rejection, anxiety, depression, and torment suddenly rushed through my entire being. The large pit in my stomach that I thought I had left behind forever was now even bigger. To say I was in disbelief at what had just happened was an understatement. How could someone be so loving, tender, respectful, funny, and charismatic to other people and yet be so obviously void of a heart? How could a human being do that to a helpless animal, especially when there was an array of other options? I don't know whether I was more disgusted by the act alone or by both of his sons' lack of response to what he had done.

Suddenly my perfect fantasy world came crumbling down, and the subsequent days that I spent with these three "strangers" began to give me a cold chill. I began to feel I might be worse off than I had been when I was at home with my mom. Our puppy was never mentioned again, which made the subject even more uncomfortable to me.

I started to pay attention to what was going on around me more closely. I started to notice the boys acting as if they had been brainwashed, to the point that they never disagreed or talked about anything that didn't praise or build up their dad's ego. He would become angry at them if they didn't respond to him with the words "yes, sir." I began to wonder if it had always been that way, and whether or not I had been blinded by my own selfish need to feel love and acceptance. My mind simply couldn't comprehend what my eyes were seeing, and confusion set in even more when the next events took place.

One evening we were all in the kitchen together; I was tired from work and very hungry. I didn't know what caused my former teacher's anger on that night, but all of a sudden I found myself slapped in the face so hard that I actually landed on the floor. His slap was then followed by a strong command never to "go against him again," especially in front of his sons. I literally had the sense slapped right out of me, and a light bulb finally went on. I had become so content with their affections and his attention that I couldn't see that I had fallen right in the middle of a possessive, controlling, brainwashing, and submissive relationship. You see, my spirit had become so broken as a child that living anywhere that was not my home seemed great to me. At this point I would find myself praying for relief and asking God for a miracle or a sign that He was still with me. When I got slapped and felt this man's rage toward me, I knew that, with my innate independent personality, things would only get worse from that point on. I remember quickly questioning myself at that point and wondering what was going on inside of my heart.

Was I so starving for love that I would willingly compromise who I was to become a submissive "little girl," eagerly waiting for the tiniest glimpse of a feel-good moment now and then to give me happiness? Today, now that I am in a different stage of life, so many things come to mind when I think back to that moment. While everything seems so clear now, at that time I was so confused and broken that I didn't even know where to turn for help or what to do.

Throughout the course of the next few months, I endured still more abuse, always followed by apologies and pleas for me not to leave because, he swore, it "wouldn't happen again." The worst part was that even though they knew I was growing more and more frightened, this man's sons only justified his actions. They told me he was only fighting with me and hurting me because I didn't know "my place in the household" and because I spoke my mind and my opinions too often. They said that if I would just stay quiet and not have such a strong opinion—about things like the "disposal method" of our pit bull puppy—he wouldn't have any reason to lose his temper and hurt me. Countless nights I tried to sleep on the sofa, only to be physically yanked back into his bed. No abuse took place while I was in his bed trying to sleep, but my fear of him had become great enough to keep me awake, essentially "sleeping" with one eye open. To say that I know what hell feels like might not be an understatement, because, boy, was I living it during that time! The only time I felt comfort was when I was either at work or in the bathroom.

In between the hellish encounters with this man, though, I did experience some feelings of normalcy. As long as I was quiet, didn't express my opinion, and acted like "everything was good," things went smoothly. But I knew I couldn't live in such an environment for long, so I began to look for a way out or another place to live. I wasn't eating much during this time, and I began to look sick. I think I only weighed 100 pounds—soaking wet.

Even contemplating leaving my current situation was hard for me to imagine—because I truly had nowhere to go. I kept wondering, *Where the heck can I go from here?* After a few more situations in the home that became very

"extreme," my feelings became almost paralyzed,

putting me into a state of almost-constant and

overwhelming panic, anxiety, and helplessness.

The violence escalated from that first slap to him

physically lifting me and throwing my body across

the room numerous times. I often prayed, *God, are*

You even here? What should I do? Have I now lost Your

protection over me?

My thoughts were all over the place, and I

finally decided to just do the formerly unthinkable

and attempt to return to my mom's house. I still

felt like a little girl, even though I had been living

a woman's life. I understood finally that I had

never been given the chance to grow up or reach

a normal kid's life milestones at an appropriate

age. I had been forced to grow up far too soon,

and this was not the life I'd signed up for. I'll

never forget December 22 of that year. I was

eighteen, finally at the legal age when I could make my own decisions. I begged my former teacher to take me back to my mom's house. I told him that I hadn't been feeling well and that I just wanted to see my sister. I told him I would be coming back, even though I had no intention whatsoever to return to him. I knew how to say all the right things to cause this man to believe me and finally take me back to my mother's place.

As I prepared to leave, I prayed desperately for a sign from God that I was making the right decision. I packed a backpack, leaving most of my belongings behind, and as we boarded a train bound for Queens, New York, I didn't even look at this man. That entire trip felt like an out-of-body experience to me—I was so frail and undernourished that I looked like I was only about fourteen years old. On the train, I started daydreaming of what the reunion with my mom would be like. I had had no contact at all with her for the past two years, not since I had left her place. In the movies, when runaways return home and are reunited with their parents, they almost always find love, apologies, laughter, relief, and thankfulness. Their family usually exclaims, "We're so glad you're back!" or "Where have you been all this time?" and so on. So many hopes and possibilities of a happy ending to this nightmare were what kept me on that train—with truly unrealistic expectations of something wonderful about to happen in my life after so many years of misery.

My state of my mind at this particular moment was one of total dysfunction. It seemed to me that the miracles I had once been sprinkled with had now found their way to others in need. I felt abandoned, alone, and helpless, and I just wanted to learn where I really belonged. At times,

I actually began to feel that I had brought this all upon myself. Maybe I *was* too opinionated, or maybe I *was* a little too independent and ambitious. Maybe if I had just been different, I could've been loved—truly loved. The idea I had about what I would feel when I returned to my mom's house and what actually occurred were so drastically different—and that was something I was *not* expecting to encounter.

My AHA Moment:

For much of the two years I lived with my former teacher, I thought it was going to be an awesome experience. I had no idea that, toward the end of our relationship, he would turn out to be an extremely abusive person, or that he would turn on me with such violence. Even when that happened, though, I knew that life *had* to be so much better than that, and I knew that at that point I was just settling for whatever I was given. Being young, naïve, vulnerable, and insecure kept me in that place much longer than I should have stayed. I didn't know how to live out on my own—I had no idea whether I could even get an apartment on my own. As a result, I felt trapped where I was for most of the time. Now, as an adult looking back on that experience, I'm actually thankful that I went through all of this, because it taught me so many life lessons and it now allows me to impart the wisdom I gained into the lives of young girls today. I want to help the young women I now mentor to make sound choices and not to put themselves in situations that could go very wrong for them. In my own life, I have forgiven and released my former teacher from any guilt, offense, or hurt he caused me so long ago, and I can now look back at this part of my life as just another learning experience.

Your AHA Moment:

Have you ever experienced something traumatic emerge from something that had originally been meant to fix a different, initial problem? Have you ever found your situation going from bad to worse and not know how to escape the situation? Have you ever run to someone for help, only to have that very person betray and abuse you themselves? Take some time to think about these questions, and search your memories for any times when you might have felt any of these things; then begin to let go of it. Write down your feelings and turn to the truth of God's Word about you and the situation.

_____

_____

_____

Who saves me from my enemies. You exalted me above my foes; from a violent man you rescued me.

Psalm 18:48 NIV

For he has not despised or scorned the suffering of the afflicted one; he has not hidden his face from him but has listened to his cry for help. The LORD is a refuge for the oppressed, a stronghold in times of trouble.

Psalm 22:24 NIV

During this time, I held on to the book of Psalms as my personal lifeline. When I hit rock bottom in 2014, the only thing that could begin my healing process was the Word. No person or counselor— nothing or nobody else—would do. I had to allow God to minister to me with His Word.

I now know that the Lord is always with me, and I have believed the many statements in the Bible that mention that our cries do not go unheard to Him. The Lord will exalt us above our foes and rescue us. These truths have provided me with so much comfort in the difficult times of my life and have given me an understanding I never knew was possible.

Turn the *Light* Back On

8

Welcome Back Home?

Have you ever had a dream or, more so, a nightmare, that was so real to you, you woke up with the strong emotions of feeling as if it had *just* happened to you in real life? Did it take a while to shake the nightmare off after you awoke? Well, I really wish that in the next part of my life that was the case— that I could have awakened from the living nightmare that became my life.

When I finally arrived at my mom's house, I went into my old bedroom and collapsed on my bed, face-down. I didn't know where my mom was, and my mind wasn't sharp enough to realize what might be going on. I was still in such shock, paralyzed by what I had just endured with the

Turn the *Light* Back On

teacher, and all I wanted to do was sleep so that I would not have to think about my situation.

What happened next became one of those experiences that I soon suppressed so deep down inside me that it wasn't until I decided to write this book, that I even told my husband about it.

I was attempting to sleep, lying face-down, when suddenly I heard the bedroom door slam shut and the sound of a lock clicking into place. I then felt someone place their hands over my mouth, covering it and whispering "Shhhhh" in my ear while forcing their weight down on me at the same time. The force that was pressed down upon on my small, frail body made me feel as if I truly was about to die. My initial thought was, *this is a setup! my former teacher is so pissed off that I decided to leave him that now he's come back to kill me!*

But then I felt my pants being yanked down, right off of my bottom, and very abruptly,

102

my body was penetrated. The thrusting that took place felt angry, violent—and desperate. The fighter in me, deep inside my mind, could envision me turning around and snapping the perpetrator's neck, but neither my will nor my body had any energy at all, and so I decided to just endure it until it was over. I thought I would die, and just be put out of my misery. What else could go wrong in my life? This was my "welcome home" experience? I thought this was going to be my *end*!

When I heard the man's voice begin to speak, I suddenly thought, *Wait a minute, this voice and its tone is unfamiliar to me. Why is this unknown person speaking my name over and over? What is going on?* When I caught a glimpse of his hands holding my wrists down, I saw light skin and hairy arms. My former teacher had caramel-colored skin. *So who in the world was doing this to me?*

I suddenly felt like I had been dropped back down into hell again, but this time I knew I was finally going to be taken out! I remember the attack finally ending with a sharp shove against my back as the man crawled off of me and left the room, slamming the door behind him.

My legs were damp, and the sheets were very sticky. When I looked down at myself, I saw blood everywhere and the man's semen on the bedsheets. I was so grossed out, and one of my first thoughts was that my body had just been forcefully shocked into getting its period. I was so disgusted that I wanted to throw up and cry uncontrollably—both at the same time. I cried there in the bedroom for a very long time—but quietly, as I didn't want whoever the man was to hear me and come back in to do that to me again. I was in shock, and I felt disgusted, violated, and dirty. I wondered why I was even alive at this point. What possible good could ever come from this? Had I been put on the earth only to suffer all the time? *Why, God? What have I done that was so terrible as to deserve this? And what's coming next? How will I be able to use this experience for any good at all, God?*

I finally got up from the bed, only to find the bottom of my pants (and the panties inside them) down on the floor. My mind could not understand why anyone would do this to me, who would have done it, and why it would have happened at my mom's house. Where was she? Why did I hear several voices outside of my room? Who was out there? Were they laughing at me? Had this attack been planned or encouraged by my mom, or was this a sick attempt to "welcome me back" to my childhood nightmares—only this time in "adult mode"? Clearly I was confused, because I don't think any of that could have been possible. But I was in a state of shock! I felt discarded, worthless—and guilty. Should I have just stayed in my mom's home to begin with, despite the abuse that had been taking place? Was this God's punishment on me for searching for love in the wrong place? Hadn't the outcome of my time with the teacher been punishment enough? What had I done that was so terrible to have caused so many terrible things to happen to me?

The next thing I remember was hearing my mom talking to someone right outside of my room—and they were talking about me! I heard my mom say that she'd thought I'd been strung out somewhere on drugs for years. And I heard her say that I looked like I was dying from AIDS. All these things that sounded like they were coming from my own mother's lips left me feeling so empty inside, and I resolved that I was done!

As a matter of fact, I was *so* done in, I felt like a rag doll available and at anyone's disposal whenever they felt the need to inflict pain or suffering on someone else.

At this point, I was simply ready to kick the bucket. Memories of childhood experiences that I had filed away in the "I resolve that this will never happen again" area of my brain, began to resurface, and I knew I couldn't stay at my mother's place much longer. To make matters worse, my mom introduced me to her new husband—and it was obvious that he was the one who had raped me! I knew it the moment we met, in his attempt to avoid any eye contact with me. I hesitated to look over at his arms, but when I did, there they were: the light-colored hairy arms that had once held down my own wrists.

I honestly felt like I was staring at the very face of the devil himself. At our introduction, he nodded strangely and he spoke my name in a low tone that sent chills down my spine.

Needless to say, I *knew* that I could not stay there for any length of time, so I had to once again determine to save myself. My immediate plan was to return to the teacher and apologize for leaving him; I would stay with him, buying myself some time to craft a more permanent escape plan. To say I had any hope left for a miracle would have been a joke. I was simply living to exist. I was frail, I was weak, and I had no willpower and no self-esteem. I was broken beyond words. At times, I even wondered if God knew me, if He even remembered He had made me. I wondered if I had disappointed Him so badly and whether that was why He had allowed so many bad things to happen to me.

Still, even though I felt I was at the lowest point in my life, the fighter in me, the type-A personality, the strong and independent young woman whom I knew was deep down inside of me, began to surface. I began to search for God in a truly desperate way. I used all of the energy I had left to seek His face and His will. All I wanted was to feel His presence. I had been baptized as a little girl, raised as a Catholic, and went to church with my cousin and her mom every week. I even attended catechism classes on Wednesdays during school hours, and I had already experienced my first communion. From the outside looking in, I seemed to be growing into a normal, loved, and well-rounded young lady. And although life had repeatedly tried to break my spirit, I mentally talked myself out of the self-doubt, and still hoped for a miracle. I prayed with everything within me for a positive change in my life, for a glimpse of true hope.

My AHA Moment:

At some point in each of our lives, we begin to realize that not all good things happen to good people. Bad things happen, too. But bad things happen to us all. No one is immune from the trials, obstacles, and challenges that this life brings. While back then I felt like I was slowly losing my identity and I was totally confused as to who I was and why I had even been born, deep down I knew there was more to my life. I knew that everything I had been going through *had* to be meant for a reason. Although my attempt to go back home hadn't turned out to be an ideal experience, I knew that the violation that took place somehow would not scar me forever. I have always had a positive outlook on life and I knew that if I wasn't dead, I still had a purpose in this life. I just hadn't yet discovered what that was.

Your AHA Moment:

Have you ever tried to go back and fix something, or revisit a situation, that deep down inside you knew was hopeless or not worth the trouble? Were the consequences ultimately worse than they would have been with not trying at all? Have you ever been violated but kept it to yourself for fear of not being believed, or of being shamed or judged? The moment you can speak the truth out loud and begin to talk about it, your healing will begin. Write down anything that comes to mind in answer to these questions, and if you need to seek additional help, please do so! Your life is worth the effort it takes to ask for help—and your future may depend on it!

_____

_____

_____

I praise you because I am fearfully and wonderfully made;

your works are wonderful, I know that full well.

Psalm 139:14 NIV

This particular verse made me feel empowered, as

if I could lift someone up myself and remind

them that God loves them right "where" they are

and "how" they are in their lives.

9

Going Too Fast

A s I made my way back into the teacher's household, I knew that my stay there would be short-lived, because I was ready for a new beginning in my life.

Still, my mind kept replaying all of my unfortunate childhood memories—and everything that had led me up to this point. I realized that I had masked all of the hurt I was feeling, and that I had made myself believe that the things I had experienced were actually "tolerable." Upon my return to the teacher, he told me that he loved me and was glad I was back; he hoped I would stay with him forever. But this time, all I heard was "*blah, blah, blah,*" and I realized that his words were meant as a trap. I was so over the lies and the abuse at that point, and I knew it was my time to take action and find a safe place for myself—by myself! I asked around to try to learn my favorite aunt's whereabouts, and eventually I made arrangements to stay with her in White Plains. I left my former teacher's household very calm and collected. I timed my departure for when I knew no one would be home, and then I left and said, "Bye-bye forever."

In reality I was thrilled at this turn of events. This aunt of mine was the one who had always rescued me from the grip of my mother in such a loving and protective way. She had not known where I was staying, mostly because I did not want her to be forced to lie to others or compromise what she knew about my whereabouts. Yet not one time did she ever speak badly about my mom. It was as if she knew I was her "assignment" in life, and she always showed up to complete the homework!

When I first arrived in White Plains and to her household, I don't recall talking much. I was deeply processing my life to that point, and I was just happy that I'd finally found peace after so many years of running and feeling out of place. My aunt wasn't a very verbal person, and part of me thought that she might not really want to hear everything I had gone through, because it might hurt her. Instead she saw fit to just leave me alone and let me heal on my own. Deep inside she might have sensed that I had a lot to process. At this time in my life, my whole world had become so confusing and turned upside down that I didn't know whether I was coming or going. I had so many unanswered questions about my life. I sometimes wondered whether my mom cared if I even existed. I questioned whether my sister might have resented me for leaving—maybe even hated me, because who knew what she'd had to endure while I had been gone. I was so relieved to have finally found peace in my aunt's house, but I didn't want to impose in her life, so I knew I wouldn't be there too long, either.

Being out on your own in this cruel, oftentimes judgmental world can be hard for some people. I found myself lost and looking for ways to fill my time so I wouldn't have to sit still and think through or process my pain. I felt like a little girl who had become trapped in a woman's body, because I had no idea how to live alone, to pay my own bills, or to simply function in society in general. But I knew I was tired of running, and I was looking forward to settling down on my own.

I was eventually able to secure an apartment for myself in the Bronx, on

McCormick Avenue. The apartment came to me unexpectedly, because I hadn't really been looking for one yet. So there I was, a "big girl" in my early twenties, working at Citibank in Washington Heights, New York City, and starting to get acclimated to my environment. Until this point, all I had known emotionally was abuse, rejection, confusion, self-hatred, abandonment, loneliness, and fear. I was ready to begin to live a happier life and enjoy the simple things that many people often take for granted—such as peace, for one.

While I worked at this bank, I also held down several other jobs: one at an insurance office and one for a modeling company.

I think I accepted the modeling gig because I still had a strong need to feel validated. My soul felt empty and broken, and my hopes and dreams had been shattered. I had no example to look to for how to achieve the American dream,

nor had I ever witnessed an example of a truly
functional family. The modeling job presented
itself just when my ego needed it. But a few
strange instances took place during this time in
my life. I was doing so much busy work that I was
wearing myself out. Being gripped by constant
fear and combining my state of mind with a lack
of good judgment often led me into difficult
situations: I was once held up and robbed on the
Number 4 train, and later held at gunpoint for yet
another robbery. I eventually finally realized that I
was just worn out, depending on too many
worldly things for validation. At that time, I
decided to simplify my life. I worked those three
jobs for a good year before finally quitting work at
the insurance company and at the modeling
agency.

As I settled into my apartment, I bought
some furniture at Pier 1 Imports to make the

small basement studio feel cozier. As if being held up at gunpoint twice wasn't enough, though, during this time, I also experienced one of the most frightening health scares of my life.

One evening after work, I was in my apartment watching TV when suddenly I felt freakishly hot and cold flashes run throughout my entire body. I was dizzy and felt cold and clammy. I grabbed my flip phone, but then it dawned on me: *Who would I even call?* I had not been on the social scene for a while, my mom and I weren't on talking terms, and my aunt and uncle were away on vacation. I dialed 911 as I tried to make my way to the bathroom, but then I fell. I must have passed out with the phone still in my hand. I'm so thankful that I had dialed 911 before I passed out, because the paramedics came to my house in an ambulance. They spotted me through a tiny basement window and were able to enter my apartment through the basement door, which coincidentally I had not fully latched.

The next thing I remember was people grabbing me, taking my vitals, and opening my refrigerator and grabbing a gallon of water, trying to force me to drink. They kept repeating the words, "She's dehydrated!" At the hospital, I learned that my kidneys had become infected because I had not been drinking the proper amount of water.

And then—as if being held up at gunpoint twice and taking a sudden trip to the ER wasn't enough—a few months later, as I was driving my older gray Toyota Camry, I was caught up in a major, several-car pileup that should've really taken my life. I'll never forget the day—it was September 22, 2000, and I was driving very fast on the major Deegan Expressway, when all of a sudden I was hit from behind by a Dodge

Durango that was also going about 65 to 70 miles an hour. I was going fast at first, but I tried to slow down as I saw an upcoming traffic jam. It was too late, however, and the impact from behind sent my car flying forward and crashing into other cars.

When I later saw the photos of my car, the trunk was literally inches away from the back of the driver's seat. I don't know how I survived—but that seems to be the story of my life.

After the accident, I was rushed to the hospital emergency room—again—in an ambulance. There was blood on my knees, and I had extreme chest and neck pain, but all I ultimately walked away with was a scratched-up knee and multiple contusions in my chest.

After a few months of physical therapy for my back and neck, I was back on the road again driving shortly thereafter. But it took me quite a while to get over the fear I felt every time I had to press the brakes on the car. I was soon able to go back to work at the bank. I had gotten the hint and had begun working only one job by that time. I had a few work friends and acquaintances, as well as quite a few clients, and we would all go out weekly to have a good time.

On one of those nights out, I met a nice guy who was very charming; all the ladies loved him, and my competitive nature kicked in. I decided I had to have him. We started hanging out within the group a lot, but we also really enjoyed hanging out together. There weren't any fireworks in this relationship, but I was finally having fun and experiencing a somewhat romantic relationship in a safe atmosphere.

After three years had gone by, all the fun outings, dance parties, and social functions came to a screeching halt when, at age twenty-seven, I found myself pregnant with my first child, a son—by a married man. Fear of commitment to a "real" relationship had allowed me to be okay with this situation. When we discussed our expectations about life with a baby, I told him that he didn't need to stick around—especially since he was already committed with a wife. I wasn't really comfortable with deceiving a woman who still loved him very much. He was just being a player. And so this moment in my life came with quite a few lessons and a whole lot of growing-up that I had to do. It was also one of the most liberating times of my life, though, because I had begun to realize that I had to be accountable for my own actions and face the resulting consequences responsibly.

My AHA Moment:

I learned so much during this phase of my life. I realized that I was moving too fast for my own good. The light bulb really went on in my head when I realized that trying to do too much at one time caused me to burn out easily and quickly. That was why I hadn't been alert at the train station, why I had passed out from dehydration after not drinking enough water. I also realized that, in an attempt to move on from my past and suppress it, I had chosen to make myself overly busy every waking moment of my day. I would multitask so I wouldn't be able to think about anything from my past. That wasn't a healthy coping mechanism at all. But I was also beginning to see that life could be fun and that I could have a good time and not feel guilty for being happy, although I was still counting on superficial things to fill the void I had deep inside.

Your AHA Moment:

Can you relate to anything I went through during this phase in my life? Did you ever hold down simultaneous jobs and keep yourself extra-busy to mask any pain from your past or to numb your mind, heart, or feelings? Or did you do anything else that you now know you shouldn't have, as a result of not wanting to deal with things that had happened in your life? Take some time now to reflect, and then jot down what comes to your mind.

_____

_____

_____

Such a person is double-minded and unstable in all they do.

James 1:8 NIV

At this time of my life, I certainly was unstable. I couldn't keep my mind on one thing without jumping on to the next thing, and I spent a great deal of time rushing from one job to the next. This was the period of my life when I had the most number of accidents and situations I caused for myself; and it was all due to my lack of focus. This verse now reminds me to take things one at a time and stay focused, so as to achieve good, safe results.

10

New Beginnings

When I was pregnant, I decided to get out of the banking scene for a little while, so I secured a job at a church—Marble Collegiate Church—and resigned from my job at Citibank. I worked as the executive administrative assistant to two pastors at the church in New York City. I loved everyone there, and they treated me with respect, value, and love. I was overwhelmed with feelings of gratitude as I reflected on the things that I had overcome in life thus far. I also realized, funny enough, that the only "inconvenient" thing in my life at that time was taking the train to and from work.

Expecting a baby and riding the NYC transit system was not a good combination. I would sometimes be left to stand on the train

without being offered a seat, and one day I
actually passed out in the very hot and crowded
train car. After I had fallen and came to, I found
that everyone had cleared out and so I laid down
across an entire bench until I finally reached my
stop.

While working at the church, some
exciting events took place for me. First, I was
privileged to sing with the Marble Collegiate
Church Choir as we performed as backup singers
in a concert by Mark Anthony, Michael Jackson,
and Toni Braxton at Madison Square Garden.
And then, Sandra Bullock's RV was parked in
front of our church for weeks while she was
filming the movie *2½ Weeks* with Hugh Grant—
everyone said that I looked like her.

In addition to these exciting events, I was
given the responsibility for all of the behind-the-
scene preparations for Liza Minnelli's wedding.

The attendees included the likes of Michael Jackson, Anthony Hopkins, and Elizabeth Taylor, just to name a few.

At the same time, being pregnant allowed me to slow down a bit. It gave me the opportunity to nurture my love for research, reading, and writing. Quiet time was new to me, but I enjoyed it. I am a student by nature, so I began to read books about child rearing, how to nurture your first child, and raising a boy. I had a lot of "new things" going on in my life, but they were good, they were peaceful, and they felt right. Knowing that I was expecting a boy, I became interested in the whereabouts of my own father—more than ever before.

As you have already learned, I grew up fatherless, but I was determined not to make the same mistakes that my father had made. I wanted to meet my father to get to the bottom of things and learn why he had abandoned me. I was at peace about the situation though. I was not angry at him, but curious? Definitely! One day I called my father's aunt, named Lydia. I usually called her at least once a month to check up on her. After sharing some small talk, each time I called, I would ask if she had heard from my father. One day, to my surprise she said yes, and she passed along his cell phone number, although she mentioned that she was unsure whether it was still current. My heart started racing, and I nervously wrote the number down. I had known this Aunt Lydia since I was a child, and I had always asked her about my father and his whereabouts. But now that I could actually possibly find him, I wasn't sure whether or not I wanted to—or even how to go about it.

My AHA Moment:

During this time of my life, I was excited that I had finally learned to slow things down and enjoy my life. I was in awe of all the new and wonderful things that were going on now. I was expecting a baby, I had a new job at a church with people who valued me, I was singing in the church choir, and I had met quite a few celebrities. Most of all, I had learned that I might be able to finally meet my father! I finally started to believe that the best could be yet to come, and I was excited about life. I also knew that if things didn't work out with my father, I would still be okay with that.

Your AHA Moment:

Did any of this part of my story resonate with you? It's okay if your answer is no, because we don't all experience the same walks of life, but have you ever experienced a time in your life that now stands out to you as one of "new hope"?

Amidst the negative parts of your past, did you have any moments of rest, peace, and new beginnings? Writing down good things is as therapeutic as writing down negative things, because it promotes gratitude and allows good feelings to come to the surface of your mind. Write about some amazing and positive times in your life, and then feel free to think on those things and expand on those memories for a while.

_____

_____

_____

_____

I will give you a new heart and put a new spirit in you; I will remove from you your heart of stone and give you a heart of flesh.

Ezekiel 36:26 NIV

This verse became so exciting to me during this time in my life, because I felt like I was finally on the way to real healing. I felt I could love the baby who was growing inside of me—and that thought alone was so exciting. Even though I was still somewhat suppressing my past in my mind, I began to feel that greater things were yet to come, as evidenced by all the new beginnings in my life.

11

The Number You Have Reached

I was finally twenty-seven years old, but I had never met my father before. I sat, staring at the piece of paper with a number scrawled across it. Yes, I had questions. I didn't have any emotional attachment to the man, nor was I even angry that he had abandoned me. But I did have questions to ask him. And how could I possibly be hurt by someone I didn't know? I decided to just grab my phone, pick up the piece of paper, and dial the number.

For some reason, I recall my heart beating fast again, and in my mind I drew a blank, so I just hung up. After a few more minutes, I got the courage back up to call again, and when he picked up the phone, the conversation went something like this:

Me: "Hi, this is Michelle."

My father: "Ummm…" (Pause…then silence…).

Me (sarcastically): "It's Michelle, your firstborn child—at least I think I'm your firstborn."

My father: "Oh, wow, Mercy's kid? Are you serious?"

Me: "Yep! It's me!" (Another awkward silence).

Me (continuing): "I'd like to meet you face-to-face as soon as possible—like, today."

My father: "Sure! Where do you live?"

Me: "I live close to the Six Train, by the ParkChester Station."

My father: "Okay, so, let me get ready. We can meet at six p.m. on the train station platform?"

Me (thrilled but maintaining a calm tone of voice):
"Sure, I'll be there...and hey, I have on a light blue
skirt with flower patterns."

My father: "Perfect. I'll see you later on then."

Me (feeling shocked that this was actually
happening): "Okay, see you then."

 I hung up the phone, thinking, *Wow,
seriously, just like that I'm going to meet my father? The
one who was partially responsible for my existence?* But
then some strange needy thoughts flooded my
mind. *Will he even love me? Will he apologize for leaving
me? Will he fill in all the blanks and voids I've felt in my
life up to this point? Is he handsome? Or is he a bum?
Will we be able to have a relationship? Does he have other
kids? Where does he live? Did he ever wonder about me all
this time? Why didn't he ever come looking for me? Or did
he, and I just didn't know?* The questions went on
and on.

Then I started wondering how different my life might have been had my father been a real presence in my life. Would I have made all the bad judgment calls and mistakes that I had made? Would he have kept my mom from hurting me so badly? Would we have been happy together as father and daughter? Would he have taught me to value myself? Would he…would we…blah, blah, blah! My mind kept playing out scenarios of what "could have been."

Six p.m. couldn't arrive fast enough. I was feeling anxious. I paced back-and-forth in my tiny basement apartment, not sure what to think or feel. As the time gradually approached, I decided to drive on over to the train station instead of walking, because I didn't know what to expect. I didn't know whether I might need to leave suddenly. And so I parked underneath the train station and begin to walk up the stairs to the upper platform.

I remember standing on the platform there, and not seeing anyone. Some trains had arrived, and it was nearing 6:05 p.m. but nothing happened. Granted, I didn't know who I was looking for. I had been told for years that I had my father's nose, and now all I could think was, *thanks a lot, by the way.* Luckily I'd also seen pictures of him when he was much younger, so I at least had some point of reference.

And so I stood there, patiently waiting as another train passed. It was now 6:08 p.m., and again nothing happened. At this point, I began to doubt that my father actually had the courage to come and meet me. Maybe he had watched a crazy talk show where a father and his daughter reunited, and it went really bad. Maybe because of that he had changed his mind. I sat down on a bench for a moment to think.

I was about to finally get up to leave when another train neared the station. Suddenly I saw a man coming toward me with a small paper bag in his hand. He walked directly toward me, and in my mind I thought, *My goodness, that must be him!* I was a little nervous, feeling a bit like a very young girl in trouble. The man approached me, we exchanged smiles, and he glanced down at the brown paper bag.

He apologized for being a few minutes late. He had stopped by a store to buy me something. He held the bag out toward me, and again, like a little girl with two hands open toward him, I gestured to receive the bag.

When I opened it, I saw a beautiful porcelain unicorn; the colors, the detail, the very essence of it was perfect! At that point, he stared at me and said, "I would understand if you don't want to call me 'dad'," and I replied, "Good!" I invited him to go eat ice cream with me, and so we jumped in my car and went to the nearest ice cream store. The next moments were uneventful, and something in my spirit kept whispering, *Don't get emotionally attached. It's not going to happen. This is just how it has to play out.*

With those ideas and feelings swirling in my heart, I began to pray, *God, is that You, or is my mind playing tricks on me? You know I've been wrong a lot of times listening to my own inner voice.* As we were eating ice cream, my father proceeded to tell me that I had a younger sister and a little brother, and that he had other children as well, but he didn't know their whereabouts. Seriously, how does that happen?

But then I realized that, of course, if this man had abandoned me as an infant, who was I kidding? For sure he would do it to other kids. I guess he decided the children he would choose to be an actual dad to, and for whatever reason I hadn't made the cut. But honestly, it was all good to me at that point. I did not feel anything negative toward him.

After we had finished our ice cream, he said, "Well, now I have your number and you have mine, so we can keep in contact." I took that as my cue to get up and leave. We walked out to my car and I drove him back to the train station. I was able to get my two other siblings' phone numbers so I could call them, too. I thanked him for the unicorn, he thanked me for the ice cream, and somehow as I watched him climb the steps up to the train station, I knew that would be the last time I'd ever see or hear from him.

Just like that, he was gone. And I was right: Days passed and there was no follow-up phone call, no sign of him. I finally got the courage to call his number, but all that welcomed me was the message, "The cellular number you have reached is no longer in service. Please check the number and dial again." I was not surprised. I wasn't even hurt. This situation just further cemented in my soul the fact that I did not want to ever have my kids subjected to a fatherless life, not if I could help it. This interaction with my father became the pivotal point that made me make "not very smart" choices later in my life.

I reached out to the younger sister I had never met and asked her to meet me outside of my apartment. When she got out of the cab, she said, "Oh my God, you look just like Sandra Bullock!" We both laughed, we hugged, we talked, and we stayed in communication for a short while, until I was not able to reach her anymore. I also called my newly discovered little brother, and

I had so much fun getting to know him. But that, too, soon ran its course and we lost touch.

Eventually my newfound sister, who now lives in Florida, and I rediscovered each other and we now have a close long-distance relationship. I love her so much. We recently both drove and met halfway between our homes—just to watch the movie *Sisters*. We had so much fun eating junk food and hanging out together.

As far as my younger brother is concerned, neither my sister nor I are sure where he is or what has happened to him, but we do hope to reconnect with him one day. However, to this day I do not know what ever happened to my father after our one meeting. My aunt Lydia went to be with the Lord a few years ago, so perhaps the Lord didn't mean for me to know what happened to my father in this lifetime. Even so, the precious relationship I now have with my younger sister was definitely worth the short meeting I did have with my father those years ago.

My AHA Moment:

Meeting my father but having none of my questions really answered (mostly because I didn't have the courage to ask him that particular day) didn't seem to affect me for good or for bad. But perhaps I needed to grow up "fatherless" in this life on earth so that I would be forced to rely on my heavenly Father and His love. I took the feelings of abandonment I experienced throughout my childhood and young adulthood, and I anchored them onto the only One who could truly sustain me, guide me, and provide me with healing in my heart. Ultimately I wasn't devastated by not having a long-term relationship with my biological father. I was able to quickly put the situation into its proper perspective and get "my own act together," since I was about to bring a precious life into this world. Instead of focusing on what I had been missing my whole life, I began to concentrate on becoming fully prepared for the life-changing moment when my baby boy would be born.

By this time in my life, I had had a good amount of time to research this "new mom" thing. Expecting a baby had become the most wonderful, exciting part of my life thus far. I journaled throughout my entire pregnancy experience, while on cloud nine for the whole experience.

Your AHA Moment:

Did you grow up missing a biological parent in your childhood? If so, did you ever try to track down or meet that parent when you became an adult? Maybe your situation varied, but you still found some similarities to my story in your own life. Take some time now to consider any times in which you felt abandoned by a parent, or wondered why things were a certain way during your childhood. Perhaps there are other situations you have buried under the surface of your mind in which you still need to shed some light. True peace can only be found in truth, and where there is truth, there is light.

Write below what comes to mind regarding these thoughts and explore what feelings surface in your heart.

_____

_____

_____

Look at the birds of the air; they do not sow or reap or store away in barns, and yet your heavenly Father feeds them. Are you not much more valuable then they?

Matthew 6:26 NIV

These words of Jesus have always made me feel so special, and this verse helped me so much throughout my healing process. By reading it and meditating on its meaning, I was able to eventually release all feelings of abandonment by my father. I know that the choice was his to leave, and that I myself had nothing to do with that. I was chosen by my heavenly Father and put on this earth to do good things, to have children of my own, and to live a life that is blessed by God. I learned to rely on Him instead of a human parent, and I began to realize who He said I was—and know that that is who I could truly become.

12

There's Something in the Air

It was 2001, and I was having the best time of my life, awaiting the arrival of my son. His father was attentive to my needs, yet I kept him at a distance—for obvious reasons. I held no grudges against him; we all make mistakes, and despite the mistakes that we had made in our relationship, he treated me very well.

My son's due date was late August 2001— but August came and went that year, with no baby. To say I was in a hurry, though, would actually be a lie, because I was having a very peaceful and enjoyable pregnancy. I enjoyed my research on parenting, my times of reading and journaling. I listened to a great deal of classical music throughout the nine months of my pregnancy, and I frequently chose to play a peaceful "mommy and baby" CD to help calm the little jumping "jelly bean" who was still growing inside of me.

My beautiful baby boy was born on September 5, 2001. He was the most precious human being I had ever laid my eyes upon. There was finally hope in this world that had been filled with so much uncertainty. The birth of this new little baby would erase all of those negative things from my past. My new son, Joshua gave me a greater purpose and showed me what unconditional love was really like, love that I'd never felt before.

I will never forget his first well-baby visit to the doctor, which took place on September 11, 2001. I had been recuperating from childbirth at my aunt's home in upstate New York, but my doctor's appointment took place in the Bronx. While I was waiting at the doctor's office, I remember thinking that something felt "off" but I did not know what it was at that time.

My son's appointment went well—he was a thriving healthy baby, so my feeling wasn't related to his health.. but I very clearly sensed something in the air—something bad was about to happen, and I could feel it. Something about that morning was bothering me immensely, but being a new mom, I wrote it off as one of the many postpartum symptoms I had recently read about.

After the doctor's appointment, we had planned to drive back to my own apartment to pick up some clothes. Still the feeling persisted— as a quiet but strange "earth stood still" premonition. When I reached my apartment complex and got out of my car, the stillness was suddenly gone. Some of my neighbors were outside, and they were all screaming frantically.

Another neighbor stuck her head out of her window when she saw me and cried out, "Michelle! My God, you need to hurry upstairs and turn on the TV! An airplane has just struck one of the Twin Towers, and it looks like this is the start of a war!" I'll never forget her next words as I contemplated my newborn son: "The world is ending, girl! Hurry up—you need to go see it for yourself!"

When I turned on the television in my apartment, I stood there in denial and disbelief. *Clearly God wouldn't do this to me now* was all that I could think. I stared at the constant replay of the airplane going into Tower One over and over. My aunt was there, and she had to finally take the baby from my arms because I could not stop sobbing uncontrollably.

My aunt and I returned to her house, as I held on to my precious baby boy. For the rest of that awful day, tragedy after tragedy continued to unfold before our eyes. When the second plane hit and people trapped in the Towers became so desperate that they began jumping out of the windows, I had to shut off the radio and the television. I later learned that during those hours, many young adults—my own age—were making their final phone calls to their parents from where they were trapped.

I needed to get back into the bubble of my "happy place"—and quick. But that was very difficult because I lived and, in fact, had grown up so close to where the events of that terrible day had taken place. It was hard for many people: One of my friends actually lived across the street from the World Trade Center; she witnessed the entire ordeal, not on television, but through her windows while she was drinking her morning coffee. She needed psychiatric help for many years to come.

As for me, I felt that the world would never be the same, but I knew that I had to be strong mentally and emotionally. I *had* to hold on to hope—because I now had a son, a little baby boy who brought me joy beyond comprehension.

Although our country has been forever marked by the tragic events of that day, my own personal hope also arrived that month of September 2001, and for that I will be forever grateful to the Lord for His blessing on my life.

My AHA Moment:

In our lives, we all realize there will be good times, and there will be bad times. I have learned that when you concentrate on the good things you have been given, the positive things, those things that the Bible says are "worthy of your thoughts," you will have more control over your feelings. I had a wonderful pregnancy and delivery, and I was so excited to become a new mom to my beautiful baby boy. Yes, the events that took place shortly after my son's birth were terrible—but as I chose to focus on what was still good in life, I was able to maintain my joy.

Your AHA Moment:

Has there ever been a time in your life about which now, in retrospect, you can say, "That was really a good time in my life—but in those moments and days, I was so stuck on the negative"? It's never too late to give something good the place it truly deserves in your memories. Recapture some of those moments and take them back for the good. Reflect on those times and then jot down anything from your past that you might need to reframe in a more positive light.

_____

_____

_____

For you created my inmost being; you knit me together in my mother's womb.

Psalm 139:13 NIV

This verse depicts the very essence of the miracle of life. When times are uncertain, human beings can always look to the birth of a baby as a sign from heaven that God still loves the world and is there for all of us. Babies—new life—bring hope and joy back into the world and show us that the future can still be a beautiful one, despite the tragedies and difficult times that we all face.

13

The Milkman and the U-Haul

I was so blessed to be able to spend a great deal of time with my son before I had to hire a nanny and go back to work. At least my son was cared for in our home. When I returned to my job, I soon felt very disconnected with the workforce, because all I really wanted to do was stay home with my new baby boy. The only time I felt happy during that time was when I was back at home with him.

Nearly a year went by, and after experiencing more and more boredom in my workplace, I finally entertained the idea of hooking up on a blind date. I say it was "blind" because I had only decided to meet this man because our assistant manager thought the world of him and wanted to introduce the two of us. I'm not sure why she was so adamant about that: Had

he asked about me, or had I ever put out a

desperate vibe?

We met during the time my son was about

to reach his first birthday. I can't say I regret the

entire relationship with this man, because in the

beginning, he seemed very nice, almost the

perfect combination of "bad boy" and "nice guy"

wrapped up in one person. He had a "macho"

vibe about him, and of course that rebellious

attitude attracted me to him. He was young, and

he seemed strong, so I figured, *Why not give this a*

try? What do I have to lose? Maybe he's a nice guy.

For the most part, he was a nice guy—

that is, until his "true self" eventually came out.

My family didn't approve of him, even in the

beginning of the relationship, but I disregarded

their comments and warnings, along with the red

flags that I did see but ignored.

My initial thought of *What do I have to lose?* was a question that was answered in time. This relationship ultimately came with a heavy price. I became pregnant. And about that time, the verbal abuse began. Soon he was yelling at me almost daily—as he had some serious anger issues. My second pregnancy was far more difficult and much less enjoyable than my first—because I spent most of those nine months extremely upset and in emotional turmoil. The only positive times seemed to be when I could feel my new baby wiggle around in my belly.

However, by this point in my life I had learned how to better stand up for myself. This man would curse me out, and I would cuss right back at him. And when he got ugly to prove a point, I would just get uglier. But the whole atmosphere shifted for me when my adorable baby girl, Arissa was born on March 22, 2004. I was almost thirty-one years old, and I was so in love with my brand-new daughter. She seemed to just melt in my arms. When she was born, I honestly wondered what more I could ask for in life—I had two beautiful children, a son and a daughter. How lucky could I be to be their mom?

My daughter seemed absolutely perfect to me. And she provided enough spunk to both keep me on my toes and make me feel like I was on top of the world. They say that little girls are often "daddy's girls," but this one was definitely mommy's little girl. Her brother loved her right away, too. I remember how I had to be away from him for the first time when I went into the hospital to give birth to his sister. When he was finally allowed to visit us there, he looked so lost, as if I had abandoned him. I'll never forget the fullness of joy I felt at holding *both* of my children in my arms. I had never felt such great love in my entire life. It was overwhelming. And despite the man I was returning home with, I was so happy that nothing or no one could burst my bubble.

When I first became pregnant with my daughter, I was living on Chatterton Avenue, two blocks away from Jennifer Lopez's house. She lived on Blackrock, and I understand that her mom still lives in that very same house. But after our daughter's birth, her father asked us to move in with him. It took me some time to process this decision, but knowing I didn't want my children to be the products of a fatherless family as I had been, I moved in with him, but the decision didn't feel quite right to me, even at that time.

Things had seemed fine between us, back when I thought I knew him and believed that he was a nice guy. He had come highly recommended by my manager, after all. But I didn't know in the beginning, of all of his anger issues—nor did I realize that this would be the beginning of yet another nightmarish relationship, causing many sleepless nights and so much fighting. This man loved to argue about everything. He seemed jealous of my very shadow because it was too close to me. I couldn't do anything to please him.

As I mentioned before, he also brought out the worst in me. I had never argued or cursed so much in my life until I met him, and I didn't like the person I was becoming while I was with him. He would accuse me of wanting to have sex with anyone he saw me look at. Soon there was no love or respect between us, and so our relationship was ultimately doomed.

We never even considered marriage, and so I began to feel like a total loser as a mother. I had already gone through so much physical abuse at the hands of my mother and my former teacher, and now the verbal abuse was becoming more and more extreme. I was being called a "whore" for no apparent reason, the "b" word— you name it, and he called me that! It was becoming too much to bear. I started looking for any excuse to leave, finally saying to myself, *With all of the crap I've gone through so far in my life, and I'm barely thirty years old, I am not going to allow another person to mistreat me like this ever again!*

One day we began arguing because he wanted to know who I had been talking to on the phone. Then, without warning, he slapped the phone right out of my hand. I had actually been talking to my mom, trying to restore my relationship with her. At that time, we had begun to talk on the phone once in a while—but this treatment by this man came as a shock to me. I didn't leave him right away after that; in fact, I let him move all of us into a bigger apartment, because he had thought the size of our apartment was our biggest problem. Later on, our relationship might have appeared to end abruptly, but I had known for a long time that there was no hope for us—before the "phone incident" had even occurred.

Finally, one day when I got home from my job at the bank, I hadn't even set my things down when I spotted him with a nearly empty bottle of wine. That's when he said, "Who's Arissa's dad?"

If you could have seen my daughter when she was born, you would have thought he was the one who'd given birth to her, because they looked so much alike. Surprised by his question, I sat down on the sofa and responded jokingly, "The milkman did it." Little did I know that those words would ultimately end our relationship.

Michelle Kirby

My daughter's father grabbed me by my ankles and yanked me right off the sofa. He then attempted to drag me by my legs around the apartment, but I was able to pull myself up into a sitting position, and I calmly began asking him to let me go. Eventually I started pleading with him, so that he wouldn't wake the kids and cause them to see such a sight. When he didn't listen to my pleas, I finally was able to grab a lamp and hit him across the head. The blow drew a tiny bit of blood as the lamp had been cracked and was sharp. It was then that he did the unthinkable.

My daughter's father went into the children's bedroom, touched the blood on his head with his finger, and then forcefully woke her up by shoving his finger into her mouth, yelling, "DO YOU SEE WHAT YOUR MOTHER DID TO ME?" I was so upset at the fact that he had just involved the children and did that horrific gesture to *my* daughter, that by the next day I had arranged for my entire family to meet me outside of our apartment with a U-Haul to move out. Little did this man know that my son's father and his wife had secured a brand-new condo for me and my two kids to move into immediately. I was out of there—with no regrets. I was moving on to bigger and better things as a single mom, and I was not afraid or willing to look back. I had come too far at that point to let anyone destroy my life—never again!

My AHA Moment:

Having two kids out of wedlock was frustrating for me—I never thought that was something that would have happened to me—but I understand now that even things we don't expect can turn out to be great blessings in our lives. I can look back now and see that the decision to try to make things work out with the father of my daughter stemmed primarily from my desire for my children to have a father in their lives, and so I allowed myself to "settle" at that time. But I can now also see that when we "force" a situation to take place, or if we pretend that things are good when they aren't, the only outcome that it will result in is ultimately bad.

Your AHA Moment:

Have you ever forced a situation to take place because you thought you wanted it or you hoped it would be "good"? Maybe you did so out of pure stubbornness, or because you were raised a certain way and you were hoping to break a vicious cycle. How did that work out for you? Are you still reaping any consequences as a result of a bad decision in that regard?

Please understand from my story that it is never too late to make things right. As long as there is breath in your body, you have the ability

to make a change. Whether these events took

place in the past or you are facing such a situation

right now, write down what comes to mind. Then

meditate on the positive things that can still come

out of the situation or what lessons you have

learned and can put into practice to make a better

future for yourself.

_____

_____

_____

Return, faithless people; I will cure you of backsliding.

Jeremiah 3:22 NIV

This verse of scripture helped me to understand

that even when I didn't seek God in all my

decisions, and when it seemed as if I didn't have

faith, the Lord still would cure me and heal me

from the repercussions of my backsliding ways,

from the times when I knew the right thing to do

but chose not to. He is a kind and loving Father,

and He will do the same for you.

14

Moving South

I'm so glad that although some things in my life haven't been ideal, I can truly say that I have always felt God's hand on my life. He always works things out for my good, even when I make dumb mistakes. And, boy, was I not done making them!

At this point, I had been living on my own with my two kids in a beautiful, brand-new condo in the Bronx, overlooking the Whitestone Bridge and the New York City skyline. I could also watch the planes heading in to land at LaGuardia Airport in Queens. We were at peace here, and we enjoyed many movie nights and fun outings.

Being a single mom felt so good. One day, while I was on my lunch break from my job at

Bank of America, I got a call from my favorite

aunt, telling me that she was moving from upstate

New York to Greenville, South Carolina. I did

not hesitate to look at the internal job postings at

Bank of America, and there I saw an open

position for an "Assistant Branch Manager,

Spartanburg, South Carolina." A lateral move?

Could this even be happening? I was so ready to

start a new life that I immediately applied online

and soon got the call to come in for an interview.

I interviewed for this position in April

2006, and the meeting went fantastic. I got the

job! I told them I had two small children, ages

two and almost five, and I needed some time to

pack up and get things in order in New York

before moving south. So in New York, I packed

up all of our belongings and secured an apartment

and daycare arrangements through the Internet. I

made the big move on June 4, 2006, and I started

my new job just two days later. I was excited and so ready to leave all of the negativity, drama, and painful memories behind me. I figured, "Out of sight, out of mind"—but I was so wrong! I settled in, got the kids situated, and started commuting from my apartment in Greenville, South Carolina, to Spartanburg. I didn't realize at first how the daily sixty-mile commute would quickly take its toll on me. At the daycare, I was usually the very last parent to pick up their children. I was fortunate to find a new job position and soon I transferred to a bank branch just a few blocks away from the apartment I was renting at that time.

So many things happened between 2006 and 2013. And as I mentioned, I was so excited to have this new beginning in my life. If I could have done just one thing differently, it would have been not allowing my daughter's father to join us in South Carolina. I justified this decision by thinking that I couldn't take both a car and a moving truck south by myself with two kids—and the truth is that I couldn't. But I still could have explored other options. Sometimes we make bad choices to seek the familiar until we just can't take it anymore. He and I had already split up and there was no chance of us ever getting back together (at least in my mind). But he still wanted to be in his daughter's life and he didn't want to stay behind in New York. I allowed him to join us in South Carolina, but I explained to him that I had plans to only rent for six months or less, and then I planned to buy a home for me and the kids.

So we drove down to South Carolina, and I did just that. I rented an apartment in June 2006, and moved into my brand-new home in October 2006. Things got so bad in the apartment with him that I had to call the authorities several times for help. I remember one day being at my wits' end and packing up me, the kids, and all of our unboxed belongings. I moved to my aunt's house temporarily, and stayed in her bonus room for a short while until my new home was ready for closing. I would have moved in with her sooner, but I arrived in South Carolina before she did. Her home was still being built at the time. I didn't move into my new home without experiencing some threatening calls from this man, being followed and harassed by him, among other things. It got so messy! One day, Arissa's dad decided to come to the front of my aunt and uncle's home. He threatened my uncle, who is about forty years his senior. I'll never forget hearing it from my uncle, and hearing him ask why I had let this man back into my life and allowed him to move to South Carolina with us.

In my mind, I had been doing the right thing by allowing him to "be there" for our daughter. I didn't want any guilt hanging over my head concerning the fact that I took his only daughter away from him. Was it a bad choice? Looking back, perhaps it was. I think he was mostly upset that I left him with the rent bill and he still had not secured a job.

I moved into my new home, and a few months later I allowed him to come stay with us until he got on his feet. He was in an accelerated real estate course, so I knew it would only be a short stay. Why I found a soft spot in my heart to extend that invitation to him is now beyond me. I do know that I was trying to model forgiveness and grace in front of my children. Our apartment lease was up, and I did not want the guilt of potentially messing his life up further. The arguments began and soon escalated so quickly that I even feared returning to my own home. I decided not to add to the fights; I was so tired of fighting. I would just stay quiet and let him scream and accuse me of all kinds of things. Even though he stayed in the bonus room of the house, I knew it wasn't right for him to be there. When I finally had to call the police after an argument, I decided that the next time he left the house, I'd change the locks and never look back on our relationship again.

Things finally settled down some, and I remember thinking, *Now, this is the life I moved down here for!* I was enjoying my life so much at that time. I enrolled my son in kindergarten and my little girl was still in daycare. My life consisted of peaceful "me time," kids' outings, apple picking, job functions, dinners at my aunt's house, movies downtown, and a lot of pool time at my aunt's neighborhood pool. We "lived the good life" for a few years, and I had promised myself not to go back to any negative situation or get involved in any other bad relationships. I had my guard up pretty strong, and I just remained focused on my kids. I went years without dating or even being interested in doing so.

One day, when I was at the pool in my aunt's neighborhood, I looked up and saw a very interesting-looking young man staring at me. Of course, I stared right back. Something about him made me think, *He's different from the rest.* It turned out he was well-spoken, well-mannered, and cute. I continued to observe him, and we bumped into each other a lot around the neighborhood. He just so happened to live in the house right next to the pool. Fast-forward some weeks and months, we got to know each other pretty well. We kept seeing each other at the pool, my kids met his daughter, and he would speak to my aunt and uncle a lot. We were all getting along, and from the awesome conversations we were all having, I gathered this man was "safe." I just wanted to be happy and have some adult conversation. I wasn't looking for marriage just yet, because I knew that when I met "the one," I would *know*—and up until this point in my life, I had not met "the one."

We eventually started dating, and things were good—until my family and I came to realize that he suffered from an extreme case of bipolar disorder and depression. It was such a severe case that I would not subject my kids or myself to anymore, and I knew our relationship wouldn't ever move forward. Toward the end of our relationship, things got so dark that his mom and I thought he might even have committed suicide on Valentine's Day because he seemed to have disappeared for hours. He was home. When I was

finally able to get into his house, I found it
trashed, with food and cigarette butts scattered
everywhere. I hadn't even known he was a
smoker, and his bipolar depression was so bad
that "he didn't even know he smoked"! When I
confronted him, he clearly stated that I had been
making things up. I cannot begin to tell you the
mental anguish I experienced at that time. How
could I ever break up with him? What was he
capable of doing to himself? In any case, we
finally ended it and never saw one another again.
He actually said that we were just such good
friends, he couldn't stand to continue to hurt me
with his inconsistent behavior. He also said that
he could never look at my face again and not feel
the pain of losing me. So, just like that, he was
gone from my life. It was for the best. Again, God
had my back.

At this point, I was so relieved because things could've gotten really bad with that man, but they never did for me, my kids, or his daughter. Till this day, I have had dinner with his ex-wife and I still keep up with his daughter. I knew he must have been living in such torment. He was a medical professional, a PA, and he did not want to take any medication for his condition, for fear of his peers finding out. Little did he know that all of his coworkers would see me at work and speak of him, telling me how they all wished he would get some help. They felt as if they worked with two different people, and they never knew which one would show up for work on a given day. But enough of that time of my life…

Now, let's get to the most amazing, incredible, wonderful, fairy-tale, unbelievably breathtaking, and most special moment in my life.

While I was dating the PA, and when I already knew that things with him would be ending soon (around 2009), I was at work one day at the bank, when right through the door a tall, dark, gorgeous, blue-eyed, three-piece suit of eye candy walked right in. His name was Tony Kirby. I never knew I could feel such butterflies in my stomach, see such fireworks, and hear birds chirping in the air all at the same time. I know this sounds corny, but those who know me know that is the only way I can describe what I felt. I completely forgot what I was even doing at that moment. I couldn't take my eyes off of him. It was more than visual stimulation for me; my spirit felt happy and comforted just looking at him. Who was he, and where had he been all this time? I had been working at that particular branch of the bank for a few years but I had never seen him before. It turns out that the drive-through teller had made a mistake on his transaction, causing him to have to enter the bank lobby. Thank God for teller errors! A teller referral led to a conversation, which led to me sending him a follow-up postcard, which led to lunch a few years later. Our first date was at "On the Border" restaurant, and we laughed so hard throughout the meal. It felt so easy to finally just be my goofy self, and he liked it.

We dated for about a year without our kids meeting each other, and then our children finally met at a "family date night" at an ice-skating rink. Tony proposed in April of 2012, and we were married in May 2013. We did all the right things while we were courting and engaged. While dating, we read and dissected the book *101 Things to Ask Before You Get Engaged*, and once we were engaged, we went to premarital counseling at the church we attended together. We scored as "extremely compatible" on our individual assessments.

While planning the wedding, Tony didn't want me to stress out with any of the preparations, so he made sure he took care of every detail. He literally told me to just relax, that he would take care of everything and all I had to do was show up. He handmade my bouquet, the toss-away one, the bridesmaids' bouquets, the boutonnieres, the table-toppers, the wedding program, and the seating chart. Without him and my amazing wedding planner, I would've been a nervous wreck. Tony knew things weren't all that great at my job, so he wanted to alleviate as much of the burden for me. I had been going through some harassment issues at work, which left me shaken up every single day. I had been asked to comply with some unethical bank practices, and I refused to cooperate. As a result, that bank is now experiencing several large lawsuits filed against them. I attempted to hide my feelings, dealt with the pressure at work, and let that pile right on top of all the negative feelings that were already there. Truly I was happy, excited to begin a new life with Tony and our new blended family. I just wanted to concentrate on our wedding, and so in the meantime I'd drink wine every night to try to numb the pain that I didn't want to feel.

Our perfect wedding day took place on May 18, 2013. I don't have words adequate to describe the joy that I felt on that day. Never in my life had I thought that I'd marry my best friend, the love of my life. Never had I imagined that our kids would get along, that there would be no more drama, and that I would be completely happy with a man who would love me unconditionally. Our wedding day was the happiest, most joyful, fun, romantic, exciting, and emotional day of my life! The entire wedding was absolutely perfect: Our youngest son, Joshua, walked me down the aisle to the song "Marry Me" by Train, while our oldest son, TJ, was our ring bearer. Our youngest daughter, Arissa, was the most beautiful flower girl ever, and our oldest daughter, Bri, was one of my bridesmaids. We laughed, we cried, and we celebrated and blended our families under the blessings of God, friends, family, and coworkers. It was the perfect beginning of our new life together. Every single person came up to me afterward raving about the intensity, the beauty, and the pure, authentic feelings they had while seeing our love demonstrated before them. They especially loved the music and the blended sand ceremony. We played the song "Waiting Here for You" by Christy Nockels. It truly was a perfect day. At the reception, each of the kids gave a toast, starting with our youngest, Joshua. When Tony made his toast, he surprised me by announcing that he was taking me to Punta Cana, in the Dominican Republic, for our honeymoon. We danced the night away and had such a great time. Our getaway car took us to Jack in the Box for burgers; then we went to the hotel. We had a flight out the very next day at 6 a.m. Both our wedding and our honeymoon were like a storybook fairy tale, and just like that we began our happily-ever-after.

I have chosen to take a break from our AHA Moments at this point, and instead allow for reflection time at the very end of the book. The next turn of events in my life are pretty intense and best understood if you can read on without interruption.

ZZ	SINGLE Sa	S

Customer:
STACY VARDARO

L WED AM

Turn The Light Back On: unmask THE PAST to reveal your FUTURE

Kirby, Michelle

W4-S051-13-32

No CD

Used - Like New

P2-DDO-225

9780692947272

Picker Notes:
M _____ 2 _____
WT _____ 2 _____
CC _____

58004835

15

The Summer of 2014

At this point I thought there was nothing that could possibly go wrong or throw any kind of wrench in my life. I had just married the love of my life, we had blended our families together, we both had very good-paying jobs, and we owned a house, several cars, more clothes and shoes than we could ever need, and we had plenty of food. We literally lacked nothing! I was happy; therefore, I must have been clearly healed, right? I had left all of my past hurts, pains, failures, negative emotions, memories of abuse, unworthiness, shame, depression, and anxiety behind me. They were so far suppressed in my mind at that point that they could never resurface again to cause any harm, right? Wrong!

This time in my life will always hold mixed emotions for me. For starters, the personal hell I had gone through, and the hard work it had taken to get me out of it, had been more than I could ever have imagined. I could have never gotten through it all in my own strength. It took me a very long time to get the images of abuse out of my head and the negative feelings out of my heart. Being okay with the noises, songs, and words even slightly associated with those times of my life was a difficult challenge for a while. Several people came to my rescue during this time, but my husband and God were most instrumental in my comeback. I place my husband first in this list, because when I went through this particular moment, which would forever change my life, I had started to doubt God during the rough times; but still, deep in my soul, I knew He wouldn't forsake me. That is what actually kept me fighting. I was starting to believe that God had orchestrated my battles so that I could deal with the root of the problem: the inner me.

Words cannot even begin to describe the devastation that soon hit my home. It was as if I had been living in a nightmare and then woken up to write about it. I so wish that was the case, that it was all just a dream. It all began when things became too hard for me to bear at work. My husband and I had been married just a year, and he had been traveling for work, almost every week, for four years straight. He had gotten a new opportunity that required traveling when we had first started dating so I was accustomed to it, and I balanced life the best I could while he was away. But this particular day, I had had enough at work. I'd never witnessed such harassment, ill treatment, and unprofessionalism before in any workplace. Our manager was out on maternity leave, and a lot of shady characters passed through in her place, making unethical suggestions to us all daily. I was told that if I didn't comply, I wouldn't have a job for much longer. Under immense pressure, I called my husband on the phone, very disturbed. I wept in the car out in the parking lot, pleading with him to allow me to write a resignation letter. After some back-and-forth conversation, he finally said, "Go ahead and resign, baby. We will celebrate when I get home." We were celebrating my freedom from one level of hell, not knowing that I would soon find myself in my own "past self-induced hell and warfare."

So, I calmly printed my resignation letter, I gave it to the "manager of the day," and she called the district manager in to accept it. Let's just simply say that if I had been smart enough to have voice-recorded the conversation, "my name would be on that bank right now." But I was just happy to get out of there. I have to be honest with you—while I was extremely happy to do so, leaving still felt very strange. I had always been good at masking my pain, and I was used to drama. Having experienced thirty-nine years of uncertainty and only one year of bliss, my past seemed to be winning at that moment. I made some bold, courageous moves to set up an LLC and curate my own financial firm with money I pulled from my 401k. I assured my husband that this was a fantastic idea, and his love for me allowed me to carry on in my venture. I had a former business partner fly in from New York for some "entrepreneur training," and in my mind, I was "all set." There was no way I could fail! I was on top of the world. My husband paid all the bills while I got acclimated to running my business and acquiring clients. I did make some pretty awesome moves, but somehow my business venture didn't take off as I pictured it, and so I started to look for other work. At this point, however, I had come to value and cherish my free time and flexible schedule, so I did what everyone believes they want to do and I started to work from home. The grass is not always greener; it truly is just different. I learned that not all things are for all people and not all things are all that they are made to seem.

My new freedom allowed my fears to breed. I am a person who thrives on routine and structure, and I love working with teams of like-minded people, but at this time in my life, I was all alone, at home. I questioned my decision to leave the bank; I questioned my decision to withdraw my 401k; I questioned my business venture, my marketability, my future, my family's future, the opinions of others, whether I'd let down my family. Basically, everything negative that a person can possibly consider, I thought up! Why wasn't I as far in life as so many of my peers whom I saw on social media? Why was I suddenly so unhappy in my own skin? Why did I feel such a dark cloud over my life? What was going on?

To make matters worse, because my husband traveled, I didn't want to bother him with these feelings, and so I simply pretended to be "okay" when he was home. I would mask my pain, and because my immune system was so low, I began to self-medicate just to be able to function. I'll never forget the times when he would begin packing to leave town for work; I would begin to sink into a deep, dark depression. It was all I could do to appear "normal" until he left. I had never before felt so alone, abandoned, hurt, scared, fearful, depressed, anxious, confused, hopeless, and literally numb to anything that was supposed to bring pleasure in life. I had started working on commission for a home mortgage company, but I couldn't stand it any longer. They had paired me up with a guy who (to me) was a combination of all the terrible men I had ever encountered in my life. I used to shiver before going in to the office, and I knew I couldn't keep up the façade much longer. That is when I started to "work from home." My definition of "working from home" soon became "stay in bed, cry all day, and feel like a zombie from home." I simply could not function. I began to have unpleasant thoughts about my life, and that was not something I had ever struggled with before. I felt so worthless that I literally kept replaying all my failures and past occurrences over and over in my mind. I could not bear the mental images. I could not stand to be awake, I had no appetite, and I was consuming all kinds of cleansing oils to rid my body of toxins, as if to rid myself of the unclean parts of me. It finally reached the point that I had taken an entirely holistic approach to live, thinking that I would be happy when _____ happened. I had begun negatively dissecting everything I didn't like about myself, all the bad choices I had made in my life, all of my past experiences—any little thing that was wrong with me.

When I was invited to take part in a program at church called "leading ladies," that was the beginning of my desperately downward spiral. Mentally I was not in a good enough place in my life to put myself through such an intense program. The books we read in the group only opened old wounds and put my life and my past in the forefront of my mind for me to deal with. It was tough to bear, and anxiety and depression began to press down on me. When you don't deal with things in your past, they will always come back to haunt you, no matter how strong you are—or how strong you think you are. Challenging myself to continue in this program while not eating well, sleeping well, or producing any kind of real income posed a huge problem for me, because it left me vulnerable and weak. I was already depressed and experiencing all of the negative emotions I mentioned before, without letting anyone else know. I was suffering in silence, I did not tell anyone about it. I have always been the "strong one," the one whom others would come to for advice, but whom did *I* go to? No one!

Well, now not only could I not stand to be awake, but anytime I would sleep, I would have nightmares. And as if recurring nightmares weren't enough, the dreams were all different but somehow all related to my past. Every single one of them caused me fear, anxiety, panic, deeper

depression, and feelings of worthlessness. I had
no idea what I could do to get rid of these feelings
that were consuming me! My life was gripped by
constant fear, and having my husband constantly
away from home might have been one of the
scariest times of my life. At first I was okay with
his work schedule, but as my depression
progressed, I became very worried. I would
picture every worst-case scenario I could come up
with, and every noise I would hear at night I
would think the worst was about to occur. I
literally feared the night! I could not stand to sleep
or even close my eyes. I went from sleeping eight
hours a day and loving life, to going without sleep
for about three weeks straight.

Everything finally came to a head in June
2014. I had been feeling as if there was a dark
cloud hovering over my home. (If you ask
anybody, my home is a peaceful, tranquil, well-lit,

and vibrant place to be.) My aunt, who is very
sensitive to her environment, spent a few nights
in my home during this time, and she later
mentioned that she also felt something was very
"off" there at that time. My husband also began
to realize that I was not well. He noticed that I
was not sleeping or eating, and he was growing
concerned—so much so that he asked for some
time off from work. I was going through
something, but I just didn't know what it was at
the time. I kept having nightmares, jumping and
jolting in my bed every night. My husband would
have to wake me and calm me down. My
nightmares became so vivid to me, that when I
would dream I was being dragged, I would
literally fall off the bed. Keep in mind that I was
barely sleeping at this time, but when I did, it was
very traumatic.

On the morning of June 18, 2014, I
became adamant about getting this feeling out of
my home. I knew that my husband was going to
take the kids out to run a few errands, and I had
been wondering what I could do while they were
gone. I meditated and began praying and pleading
with God to put a stop to this nightmare of a life.
I waited for my husband to leave with the kids,
and when I heard the garage door go down, my
body began shaking and my heart started racing. I
felt like I was in the middle of a battle against my
past, yet it felt even heavier than that. I grabbed
my Bible, a cross with the words of Philippians
4:13 written on it, and a book from my library
that I had purchased about two years before, on
the subject of how to rid strongholds from your
life. The book had never been read before—or
even opened. I had purchased it out of curiosity,
because my church had been teaching at that time

on spiritual warfare, strongholds, and the areas of your life that could possibly be attacked if your house was not in order. Little did I know that it was a book that listed everything negative that could affect a person's life—from A to Z. It was a self-help cleansing book, and it included prayers and affirmations to experience closure on any given topic.

So, I made it my business to get this closure! I walked all around my house, praying and sometimes yelling for the things of my past to leave my life. It was a powerful experience. I went into every room of my home and spoke positive affirmations. I opened every window blind and curtain and kept praying and confessing everything I had ever done and every feeling I was feeling. It was a draining experience. I must have opened every single cabinet, door, and window shade in the entire house. I was desperate, tired of the darkness, tired of feeling depressed, and searching for clarity and hope again—something, anything that would help.

This book that had come into my life literally listed all of the things that I had been feeling, had once felt, or had been subjected to in my life. I was unmasking all of my past hurts and bringing them to the surface once and for all, and so the experience of "cleansing my house" left me extremely drained! I was still not eating, and I could not function well. (Going without eating or sleeping is not something human beings can do and "still live." Research shows that without food or sleep, the human body begins to deteriorate; it begins certain survival mechanisms, but if these patterns are kept up, it can lead to death.)

I was not consciously choosing not to sleep or not to eat; at this point I simply couldn't! I share this with you now to help you understand that if you suppress your past, mask your hurts, and choose to deny the things that have happened to you, they can have such an extreme effect on your mind, body, and spirit that you could literally die. When we think we are "okay," chances are we aren't. I had chosen to be my own doctor and therapist, and I had read so many self-help and Christian books that I seriously thought I'd been "healed." But when you have a true calling on your life (and we all do) but we are so far from operating in it, sometimes we need to be shaken to our very core so that God can pick up the broken pieces and start to mend us Himself.

16

The ER

So what better gift could I give my husband on his birthday than a wife who is going through a nervous breakdown? Well, trust me—his gift would come soon. Yes, I was completely done, or rather, *undone!* When he returned with the kids that day, the house had been turned upside down. My attempt to "air out" our home had backfired on me due to pure exhaustion. At this point, I was running on fumes. I didn't know whether I was coming or going. I could barely talk or communicate anything that made sense. My husband had to take my phone and handle all of my calls, texts, and work-related issues, but all the while he was so gentle with me. I-was unrecognizable as myself. If you would have looked at my eyes, you'd have seen that I was gone—there was no life left in me. I had begun to think that my life was truly over. What was I doing to my kids, to my husband? What—or who—had I become? Why was I so unstable? How was it possible that I could break down so dramatically after so many years of being so strong? All I could think was, *I obviously cannot handle my past, nor can I handle the events that have taken place in my life now, so I must be unworthy of even being alive. I am just taking up space!*

I had been self-medicating to try to find some relief, and again, to mask what was really going on, when I accidentally began taking the wrong pills and found myself confused at being so sleepy during the day but wide awake at 4 a.m. My life became a blur, until one day I finally asked my husband to take me to the ER. I knew that I was having a panic attack, aka a nervous breakdown. Happy belated birthday, honey! It was the day after my husband's birthday; I remember thinking the day before, *I can't lose my mind on his birthday!* Honestly, after that I don't remember having any thoughts of anything. By the time we got to the emergency room, I was a mess. My heart was racing so fast, and I felt like I was going to die at any moment. The doctor gave me intravenous liquids to rehydrate me and provide my body with the nutrients I was lacking. After running some tests, he told my husband, "She's perfectly healthy—physically. Bring her back here if the panic attacks persist or if there are any signs or concerns of suicide." Whatttttt? Suicide? Was he kidding???!!! What had my life come to?

The ER doctor sent me home with some prescription medications, and would you believe that, even after taking something that should have knocked me out and restored some kind of rest and peace to my life—I still couldn't sleep! I was literally living a hell on earth. What was I supposed to do? *God, are You even here? Have You left me completely! I can't even function. And now they are saying that I can't even come back to the ER for help unless I show signs of suicide or have another panic attack! Whattttt???*

I kept recalling these recent events in disbelief, wondering how my life had taken such a drastic turn. And, of course, with no sleep things seemed worse than they really were. Have you ever gone twenty-one days *without sleeping?* Taking little catnaps out of pure exhaustion, but not knowing the difference between night and day? As if it wasn't enough to feel completely helpless and worthless, my daughter came into our bedroom that night, crying and lying beside my bed on the floor, pleading with me to feel better.

My husband kept telling her, "Your mom is very sick, but she will get better."

Before that first trip to the ER, on June 25, 2014, I had had about five nights of restlessness, crying, screaming, praying, doubting, and yelling, and I could tell my husband had no idea what to do with me. He kept calling my aunt to try to understand what I was going through, what things in my past might have brought about my current state. My aunt responded, "Tony, Michelle is very strong, and she will get past this. But she has to go *through* it. She has a lot of things in her past that have been bottled up for far too long, and it just hit her all at once when she was the most vulnerable. She never got the closure she needed with her mom, and she never got the chance to process what she's been through in her life. She is a strong believer, and she will keep her faith. We come from a strong line of women who have dealt with these things. This is just a process she has to go through. Pray with her, even if you don't feel like it, and take her to the hospital if she needs to go. She doesn't have to want to go, but take her if she needs to go!"

I felt an internal fever, almost as if I was on fire from the inside, and I took cold showers to get some relief. My body was all out of whack, and all my husband could do for me was pray. He was so angry at God that he would just pray, "Really, God, why this? Why her?"

My husband said that when he got up from his night's sleep, he would find me praying but repeating words or phrases over and over. He was really getting angry at God, because he couldn't understand why my quest to grow closer to Him was pulling me further away from Him. The more he would pray and ask for help from God, the less he would hear from Him, until he even began bartering with God: "Let *me* have this, and I'll deal with it! Just set her free!" He yelled out to God, "If I have to hurt this badly to get close to You, and if You were trying to win me over through this experience, You are really messing this up! How could You allow someone who is simply trying to get close to You, be left out in the cold like this?"

Tony was very concerned about me at the ER, but because it all seemed like a blur to me, I had to ask him later what happened to make sure I had an accurate account. This is what he told me about that time: "Michelle, the first trip to the emergency room was one of the scariest moments for me. I was so concerned you weren't going to make it, or even worse, that you would never be yourself again. Nothing I said could calm you down. I kept going over to the doctors, asking them what was taking so long and why you were so uncontrollable. You clung to me so tightly you literally ripped my shirt. When you fell down, you hit your head so hard that the doctors came over to check on you and give you some pain medication. They even gave you Valium to try to knock you out so that you wouldn't accidentally hurt yourself again, but nothing seemed to work.

"The waiting room in the ER was rough. People kept asking me if you were okay, but all I could do was hold you so you wouldn't hurt yourself. I was very concerned because I'd never seen you in such a condition! This was at the peak of your nervous breakdown. At home, I knew something was wrong, since that night you cried for hours talking about your abusive past. You talked about your mom, your ex, and others that I had no clue had even hurt you! You kept talking about falling behind on your books for the church course you were taking. I started looking for those books to see if I could learn what might have triggered your breakdown. I was so restless because I didn't know what to do. I only took you to the ER because your aunt said that I should, and because you finally told me you needed help. I was so afraid of making the wrong decision and letting you down. At some point, my sadness finally turned into anger, because there seemed to be no relief for you. They sent us home with some medication for you and they asked me to bring you back the next day if you showed any signs of suicidal thinking, if you hurt yourself, or if you had another panic attack."

Turn the *Light* Back On

17

The Note

When I got home from the emergency room that night, I felt like I was in a fog. My mind was so strong and yet so weak at the same time. I replayed the events at the ER in my mind, and the one thing that stood out the most was the doctors saying, "She is healthy—physically. The only reason you should bring her back would be if she hurts herself or shows any signs of suicide." I had a bump on my head from when I fell, and the house was very quiet. My aunt had urged Tony to take my daughter over to her house so she wouldn't see me like this, as I only seemed to be getting worse.

I can remember that night so vividly, and I'm so thankful now that I am writing this on the other side of that experience—and that it was not part of my obituary. As I mentioned before, my home felt eerie; there was a strange feeling there, and I was scared. I hardly said a word as my husband just watched me. I went to bed and tried to get some rest, but I had not slept for over three weeks. Even the Valium they had given me at the ER didn't knock me out, and I knew that something was very wrong. Was I that afraid of ever sleeping again? At that time, I wasn't having nightmares—but it was only because I didn't sleep.

The next event was when my downhill spiral seemed to finally hit the very bottom. I could not sleep as I lay next to my husband, so I got up from the bed and went to lie down on our sofa in the living room. It was a gray sofa, and the moment I lay on it, I suddenly pictured it with my blood splattered all over it. My thoughts began to race: *My God, what are these images? Please take them out of my head!* I began contemplating my worth, and remembered how my daughter had to be taken out of her home, because I was "so far gone" that my aunt didn't want her to see me in such a state. I thought of my husband fighting with God and pleading with Him to heal me, but how I still hadn't slept or eaten a thing. I knew that my body was shutting down, and I felt so helpless. The most frightening thing happened when I found myself going into the kitchen and grabbing a small white steak knife. I was shaking, with hot and cold sweats covering my body. I kept thinking, *I love my family too much to do this to them, and I can't take my own life because it would cause them too much pain. Who would ever want to wake up to find their wife lying on a couch—dead? And my kids? There's no way I can do this to them—or to me! But wait.*

The doctor at the hospital said that if I "showed" any signs of suicide, I could get help!

So I sat there in the kitchen and typed up a "suicide note" in the Notes section of my iPhone for my husband to find and read. I don't fully recall what I wrote, but when the conversation came up later, my husband said that he deleted it, that he never wanted to read it again, and that he was adamant about never mentioning the contents of that note ever again. So I am respecting his wishes by not including here what I do remember writing.

After I finished my suicide note, I took the knife and started picking at my IV injection site, hoping to make just enough of a mess for it to appear as if I was trying to take my own life. I did not know what else to do. They had given me Valium and I was *STILL AWAKE*! I honestly felt like I was in a never-ending cycle of hell on earth.

The night was so long, and I could hear the crickets and then the birds beginning to chirp toward daybreak. I did not sleep a wink. The sun came up, and my husband eventually found me on the steps to the bonus room, wrapped in a blanket with the knife still in my hand. I said to him, "I think I need to go get help." He was very calm and he held his neutral facial expression as he realized that the situation had just shifted dramatically. When I later asked him about that moment, he said, "It was the first time during this ordeal that I saw any sign of clarity from you. You looked sad, but I also saw a sense of relief and clarity in your eyes that I had not seen in a while."

He took me to the ER and explained what had occurred. The doctor took my blood pressure and routine vitals. My husband told him that he finally had some hope, because I was actually speaking more calmly. The doctors came in and asked me a series of questions, then they asked me to change into a gown. My husband was asked to talk to a case worker, then three other people spoke to him, one of them telling him to tell me good-bye. They explained to him that they were going to take care of me from that point on. He watched them walk me back into the waiting room. He put on a brave face, said good-bye to me, then walked out. He later told me he went into the bathroom at that point and cried uncontrollably. After pulling himself back together, he walked to the car, got in, and sobbed some more. He felt like he was in a daze, and he drove around aimlessly until he found his way to our church parking lot. There he sent a private message to our pastor in the hope of asking for prayer and receiving some kind of comfort and confirmation that I would be okay.

Meanwhile, the doctors were trying to set me up in a facility that could nurse me back to health, while they watched me to ensure I'd be safe. My husband had asked if I would be kept locally. They had told him that I would be, but that he wouldn't hear any more details until I was placed. He anxiously waited for me to get settled in, but then after it got dark, he started to blow up the hospital's phone lines to find out where I was. He eventually called the facility where I had been taken, but I had not been checked in yet. When he called a final time, he pleaded so much that the lady finally told him, "Listen, I am not supposed to tell you anything. She has to be the first one to contact you. When she does, she will give you a password so that you can continue calling her, but I will tell you that she is here. She just isn't fully settled in yet." I never called Tony that night! He started imagining the worst as the hours went on.

He thought I was so upset at him that I didn't want to talk to him. He said to himself, *What have I done? Did I do the right thing? Did I wait too long? Is she angry that I let them take her away?*

I finally called him the next morning, and he was so happy to hear my voice.

Michelle Kirby

18

Crazy Lady

On June 26, 2014, I was admitted to a behavioral health center in Greenville, South Carolina—and I was placed on the worst floor possible for my situation. I was in a psychiatric ward, with people who were so far gone mentally. There I was, hoping for relief and a few days of medicated sleep to regain my senses and return to my normal life, but instead it got so much worse. I was placed in a room with a schizophrenic woman who kept screaming at me, demanding that I give her a bath and calling me every name but my own. The first night, they told me to line up with the others for my "nighttime medications," and I took what I assumed were sleeping pills. I later found out I had been given high doses of sleeping aids that should have knocked me out for days, along with a mixture of medications for anxiety and depression that should have shut down my body for a period of time.

Instead of sleeping, however, that first night in the facility was one of worst nights I would live through in my entire life! It was so bad that this time I literally contemplated killing myself. I could not function, I could barely speak, I couldn't move, I was hot and cold at the same time, I was not hungry, and my brain felt like it was about to explode. I am so lucky I did not have the energy or the means to follow through with my suicidal thoughts, but I was completely at the end of my rope. I cried for hours and hours, so long that I began losing my voice. I only wanted to sleep—and have the schizophrenic woman taken out of my room. I could not walk, because my body felt paralyzed, but my brain would still not shut off. For the first time in my life, I had lost all hope and all sense of self, and I honestly thought I'd be better off asleep—permanently. Although my insomnia was extreme, I still had enough mental clarity to wonder why I had been placed in a room with what might have been the "worst" patient in the entire facility. I couldn't fathom why, when they were told I had not slept for more than three weeks, they didn't medicate me and then place me somewhere where I could actually sleep. Were the doctors completely unaware of my actual state? Didn't they realize that if I continued in that condition for much longer, I could have lost my mind and never recovered? I know this now, because I have done extensive research for three years now, and I know that I might not have gotten out of that place alive, after entering in the state I was in.

Study after study shows that I beat all the odds—

at a more-than-one-in-a-million ratio.

I am sure that many of you who are

reading this have gone through some sleepless

nights and have lost your appetite at some point,

but this was on the other side of our normal daily

battles. I later came across an article that describes

an experiment conducted on a group of people

who were forced to stay awake. It describes the

effects this lack of sleep had on their brains. The

results of this study are not for the faint of heart.

So, back to the hellish psych ward. The

next morning, they handed me an evaluation

sheet, asking how I had slept, whether or not I

had an appetite, and whether I had any thoughts

of hurting myself or committing suicide. I

thought, *Are you kidding me?* Could no one hear

the hours of screaming and pleas for sleep I had

made that night? Or maybe I had already been

categorized as "crazy," and so they had chosen to disregard my cries? I looked down at the paper and answered no to every question, and then wrote "I NEED SLEEP!" diagonally across the page. The next two nights were even worse than the first. I did not talk to anyone, not even my counselor, and I was pissed off that the woman in my room would not shut up! I grew so lethargic that I attempted to stay in my room for an entire day. I was hoping to just be able to take a nap while my nut job of a roommate left to eat breakfast or take part in the daily activities on the floor. I just wanted to feel normal and regain some of my strength, but wouldn't you know it, they adamantly insisted I come out of my room and go to the lunchroom to eat some food, and then to take part in the activities and discussions they had planned. Just then, I looked down and saw my scrubs turning red; I had gotten my period right then and there in front of everyone! I panicked and looked at one of the staff members, while pointing down at my pants. She gestured to me and pushed against my back to put me back in the line. I had to go down to the eating café covered in my blood! When I got into the line to get my food, people laughed and kept looking at me strangely. I sat down in a corner alone, staring at my food, crying, and wishing I was dead.

I had never in my entire life wished death upon myself before, not even when I had been at home on the gray sofa typing out the staged "suicide note" to my husband. I waited for everyone to be dismissed from lunch, then I managed to find my way back to my room. All the while I was walking like something was stuck between my legs—because my pants and entire lower body were drenched in blood from my period. On the way back to my room, I eventually collapsed. I remember being put into a wheelchair; I was forced to sit in all that blood as I was taken back to my room.

I smelled like a dead corpse. I could not recall the last time I had showered, maybe it had been one or two days before, and now there was the blood. It was more than I could bear. I crawled into the shower with my scrubs on. I turned on the water, sat on the floor of the shower, and watched all of the blood run off of my body, but it wasn't "bath time"; I had apparently missed the 7 to 9 a.m. window of time for cleaning up. At that point my wacko roommate came into the bathroom, saw me, and then ran out into the corridor, yelling "Blood! Blood everywhere! Melissa is dead!" All I could think was, *My name is Michelle, lady—get it right!* I got reprimanded by the hospital staff for not adhering to the bath schedule. Luckily I then

found some clean scrubs on my hard metal bed.
The worst part of this ordeal, though, was I had
not yet called my husband to bring me any
clothes, or pads for that matter, so I had to wear
Depends undergarments to hold the huge maxi
pad they gave me in place. What a sight! My
husband came to visit me that day, and he
brought my daughter Arissa and my aunt with
him. Talking to my aunt later and hearing her
recollections of that day sends chills down my
spine, and it brings tears; to this day my eyes still
well up because my daughter was so emotionally
impacted by seeing me in that condition. My aunt
has said, "Michelle, when Arissa saw you, she
could not stop crying, and she had so many
questions. We had to sit with her outside and
explain to her that you were just being held there
until you got better. She did not want to leave
without you, and she did not want to take "no"

for an answer. She told Tony that you were in "that" room so we needed to just go take you home. We were all scared when we saw you, but she was really scared when she saw your face. Your eyes were gone. She would talk to you, but you were unresponsive, and when she cried, you did not even cry with her. She didn't understand what you were going through or why you were there. When you spoke, you told me that you had not yet been able to sleep and that the place was terrible. You mentioned some lady wanting you to bathe her, and the derogatory things you heard people say late at night. We were not happy with you being there, but we couldn't do anything about it except to wait and pray."

I can remember feeling numb that day, and watching my daughter cry while I could not shed a single tear. I will tell you that after I finally got some rest and recalled that moment, I must have bawled for hours at the thought of my daughter feeling so hurt by what was going on.

The next night was again unbelievable and unbearable. I wish I could adequately describe my fear, doubt, pain, and the sensation I felt throughout my entire body. They again, did not move the crazy lady out of my room. Instead, she kept screaming at me and watching me like a hawk. Then she said she saw things around my head and that I was looking at her "scary." Little did she know that she was scaring the little life I had left right out of me!

I remember feeling a sense of relief, thinking that maybe that would be the night I would be able to sleep, because my crazy roommate finally fell asleep. But who was I kidding? By the time I had closed my eyes for about five minutes, she started banging the headboard and talking jibberish yet again. *Are you flipping kidding me?* I thought. *Are they trying to drive me crazy in here? I'm not too far away from it! I'm going to crack! I need to speak up at tomorrow's psych evaluation and tell the Dr. what is going on, so that I can finally sleep tomorrow night! I cannot go another day without sleep! My brain can't take it anymore.*

I rocked back and forth on my hard metal bed with my hands over both of my ears, and then I lay curled up in the fetal position until the sun came up. Do the math—no sleep, going on how long now? I also had not eaten a full meal in over four weeks. I would just pick at my food and then throw up. I finally had the abs I wanted, but I despised the cost that came with it.

I got up that morning and took a shower, then put on the same scrubs. I did not know whether I was going to get better or only get worse. I was fearful of everything: the place, my roommate, the doctors, the nurses, the orderlies, and most of all, having my family see me this way again. All of these thoughts sent me spiraling down into a desperation I had never known before. When it was my turn to finally talk to the doctor that day, I drew a blank; he kept saying, "Michelle!" and waving his hand in front of my eyes. Finally he said, "Can you write down what you are thinking?" I nodded and took the pen from his hand. Then I wrote something along these lines: "Need to sleep, haven't yet, lady wants me to bathe her, she's scaring me, my brain hurts and I'm taking way too many meds, please help me, I'm really scared."

And just like that, I felt immediate relief. I cannot begin to explain it, other than God Himself gave me the strength to write out those words and allow the doctor to see that I was literally at my breaking point. From there it could have only gone a few different ways: He could listen to me and help me IMMEDIATELY, or I could have wound up completely nonfunctional for the rest of my life, or I could have been taken out of there in a body bag. I'm so glad that doctor decided to move my roommate and have the nurses keep a closer eye on me. I remember him saying that they were going to change my meds again. Then he walked me back to my room with some of the nurses and told them, "I don't know why she hasn't already cracked. This is serious. From the notes I've read from her husband, she hasn't slept in about a month. I don't know how she's even functioning. I want you to give her the strongest dose of Valium and then let her sleep for as long as she can. I know it's daytime, but she needs this, and switch her current roommate with the woman in room seven immediately."

The only thing I remember at that point was taking the meds while everyone watched, and feeling like I had been given anesthesia. I felt like

I'd been hit with a building, because I stumbled

onto the bed like a rock—and didn't wake up for

twenty-six hours! I was told I slept from 9 a.m.

until 11 a.m. the next day!

Michelle Kirby

19

Turn the Light Back On

When I finally woke up, I was so happy and relieved that I had started to feel like my normal self again—but I was very aware of where I was and all that had happened to me. Still, I was okay with it, because I was so thankful now for my life. I called my husband and told him that I had just had the best sleep of my life! I asked him to please bring me my Bible, my tooth-whitening pen, some more pj's, and my favorite (small) Lucky brand jeans. He later shared with me that "at that point, I knew my baby was back and that she was going to be okay."

I went down to eat lunch, and for the first time in almost a month, I actually felt hungry. I

was not only hungry for food, but I was hungry
for the Word. I still did not want to take part in
any of the ward's activities, especially because at
this point I didn't feel I really belonged there, but
I was kept there another five days. I just wanted
to read my Bible and journal—and so I did. I
participated in some of the activities: showering,
eating breakfast, check-ins with the doctor, some
small groups, talking about my feelings in a group,
free time, eating lunch, watching movies, group
discussions, eating dinner, and then some more
free time before lights-out! The staff had
strategically set things up in such a way that they
could control the patients' days from 7 a.m. until
ten o'clock at night; this helped patients to
reestablish a normal routine in their lives. I
participated, but I also happily went into my room
to read my Bible and journal every chance I got. I
called my husband once a day, and he would visit

one more time, this time bringing my son Joshua to visit as well. Joshua had been up in New York for a few weeks, but Tony flew and brought him home for me because I wasn't in any condition to travel. I felt as if a huge weight had been lifted off my shoulders. During my free times, I would eat, pray, journal, eat some more, and thank God over and over for not leaving me in the state I'd been in. I held on to 2 Timothy 1:7, which states, "For God has not given us a spirit of fear, but of power and of love and of a sound mind" (NKJV). That has become *MY LIFE VERSE*! Because I thought I was losing my mind, I thought the enemy had finally gotten what he was looking for. Up until the time I was allowed to sleep for more than a full day, I had felt completely defeated! My new roommate was so nice to me and said, "I have been rooting for you! I'm glad you're feeling better. Your family is lovely—that little girl loves you so much. Let's pray together." I later found out that she suffered from a mild case of dementia and would sneak out of her family's home; she wound up there as a repeat patient for a few days every once in a while.

One thing that stands out to me from those days is that the bathroom was very dark, and the light switch was outside the bathroom door. Anytime I would go in for a shower, my roommate would get up and turn off the light. I'd yell, "Hey…can you turn the light back on?" Little did I know, that was the phrase that would put me on my true journey to healing, self-discovery, a closer walk with the Lord, and a stronger foundation in my life! I would always smile when she turned the light back on for me, because I knew that every shower was bringing me closer to the day when I would go home and begin to heal—the proper way.

The next few days were filled with routine as my body gradually returned to its normal rhythms. The doctors decreased my sleep medications, and even the meds for depression and anxiety. It was now July; I was scheduled to be released on July 6, but when I had my evaluation with the psychologist on July 3, I was able to glance at the notes he was taking. I saw that he had written, "Ready for discharge, severe insomnia—corrected, sleep deprivation—corrected, loss of appetite—corrected, responsive, active in all activities, even led one of my group discussions, has made friends, and is ready to go home. Counseling follow-up mandatory and referral must be filled within two days. Sending home. NEW DISCHARGE date: 4th of July." I was released on *Independence Day*! I could also see at the top of the page where he had made notes during a conversation with my husband about my condition; he had written the words "Spiritual warfare?" and circled the phrase. At the close of our conversation, he looked me in the eye and said, "I am approving you for an early discharge so that you can go spend time with your family for the holiday. I think I know what really happened to you. I'm a believer, and I don't think you ever have to worry about a relapse, Michelle—but I do highly recommend counseling for your healing process to start."

I was so excited! I called my husband and for the rest of the evening I was on cloud nine. I was so ready to get out of there! One of the young girls who worked there said, "Hey, I hear you're leaving tomorrow. I'm gonna miss you!" I took one more shower before dinner, and yes, my roommate turned the light off—but that would be the last time anyone would ever "turn my light off again!" I had been given another chance to live, to heal, to seek my God-given purpose, and to run toward the only Light I ever needed to be whole again, my Lord and true Savior, Jesus Christ!

Was it going to be easy? I didn't think so, but I was ready to go at it with everything I had, and I was determined to enjoy the process and the journey ahead so that I could someday help others who had faced the same thing.

My AHA Moment: I had finally come to the realization that in order for me to truly live a happy, fully authentic life and be healed, my journey was just beginning. I realized that I had to lose my ego and my pride in order to gain my true self, and that I had to continue the process of healing with help, being unashamed and open to finally processing everything I had gone through in my past. I had to let it go, releasing all the feelings associated with what had happened. I was coming to the end of my old self and moving into a new life, a life in which I would find my real self, as the woman whom God had created me to be.

Your AHA Moment: Have you ever felt that you were at the end of your rope? That you did not want to continue putting any effort into life? Perhaps you even contemplated taking your own life due to such extreme desperation. Have you ever feel unworthy, worthless, or panicked because you could not sleep? Did you ever experience any of the things I went through, and did you wonder how you would ever get out of it? Did you think, *Is there hope for me? Do I even have a purpose?* Well, now is the time to take a final inventory of your life. Really reflect on your past and check to make sure you no longer have any of these feelings or thoughts. If you do, please seek help. Take some time to pray now about this, and write down anything that comes to mind. Or you may go directly to Appendix A and seek out one of the hotlines listed there. Your life matters! You have so much to offer this world, and you are important! Be strong and unashamed, and know that your best days are truly ahead of you. I love you, and I am so thankful that you have shared my journey with me. Now it's time for you to start your own journey, no matter where you're at in life.

_____

_____

_____

The LORD is my light and my salvation—whom shall I fear? The LORD is the stronghold of my life—of whom shall I be afraid?

Psalm 27:1

This verse says it all: The Lord is my Light! He never left me alone, even in my times of deepest darkness. He is the stronghold of my life, and I now have no negative thoughts. I fear nothing, for I have Him inside of me and that is all I need. My relationship with Jesus, my faith...it saved me.

My Journey to Now

- Participated in many counseling sessions with doctors, mentors, and pastors…

- Returned to the workforce in February 2016…

- Became a lifestyle blogger for Insouth magazine…

- Obtained LifeCoach Certification through ICF…

- Became a life coach (see michellekirby.me)

- Began serving on Inside Redemption Television…

- Auditioned for a news broadcast station

- Invited and enjoyed a consecration weekend...

- Volunteered at middle schools to speak with young girls...

- Started a youth ministry...

- Founded a 501C3, Become Ministries...

- Emceed an inaugural event for a magazine company...

- Featured in a local magazine's summer edition swimsuit issue...

- Attended countless powerful conferences, including Straight Out of Excuses, with Real Talk Kim, three 212 conferences at my church (in 2015, 2016, and 2017), and other women's conferences...

- Attended Kingdom School of Ministry in July 2017, now graduate of KSM 2017...

- Began on a path to becoming ordained as a pastor…

- Traveled a lot…

- Restored relationships…

- Knitted new relationships with sisters who love me…

- Started writing my first book…

- And most important, have become fully healed and am living an authentic life fulfilling my purpose…

Conclusion

No matter what you go through in life, *you* are important, and you can and will find your purpose and live out your destiny, if you seek good things. Material things will come and go; accolades and people being pleased by what you do is unimportant. Are you fulfilled? Are you living out your life with a pure, healed heart, and are you being the love you want to see in this world? Those are some of the questions that I began to ask myself, and my answers weren't what they should have been. But now I am humbled that God would use my life to share with others in hopes of helping them to break down barriers, to vanquish the misconception that we are defined by our past and that there is no way out. That is so far from the truth! We all have an innate desire to be good, to do good. Whether you are a believer or not, curious about God or not, you still have goodness in you, and you have so much potential inside of you.

Are you living in truth? Have you begun to search for your most authentic self? The truth really will set you free. Dr. Cindy Trimm (world-renowned spiritual life coach, world shaker, CEO, and my life coach and mentor) once said during a coaching session, "Truth is light! When you find your place of truth, you will find your place of dreams, potential, authenticity, and the hidden talents that are inside of you!" That resonated so much with me, because that's why I am so happy even after *everything* that I have been through. Who doesn't want to be happy in their own skin? You must dig deep down inside and ask yourself some questions, and then be willing to go through the process of becoming the best version of yourself! You owe it to yourself!

Ask yourself, Whom was I meant to impact? Have I been called to write a book or otherwise start sharing my story to help free other people? What can I do that will leave a positive impact in this world? With your story and your life, you can save so many others, and I truly believe that. I believe in you!

When you find your place, you will feel it, and you may need to make the decision to tackle some tough issues that may be at hand in order to start your journey to self-discovery and healing. But it's never too late. We never stop learning and attempting to become better people daily until we take our last breaths on this earth. So I encourage you to be truthful to yourself and make sure you are healed, so that you can have the energy, courage, capacity, and foundation to do all that you were meant to do! If I can do it, you can too! We all have gifts that, when explored and tapped in to, lead us into a life of endless wonder, joy, purpose, meaning, fulfillment, and peace. This book should have given you a lot to chew on, but when you realize that you aren't alone and that there are many resources out there to help you find true happiness and rid yourself of the dark shadows of your past; there is *nothing* you can't accomplish!

Still, it is entirely up to you to unmask your pain, reveal the hurt, and turn the light back on in your life! Live again, dream again, be happy again, be motivated, be inspired, and laugh again. You hold the light in your hands! Will you flip on the switch? I now seek life with passion every single day, because I know who I am—flaws and all. I strive to be better daily, and I walk in alignment with my purpose. God has allowed me to take my *mess* and turn it into a powerful *message* to empower others. And my passion is now to help others see the light and have their own AHA Moments. Thank you for sharing this journey with me. Feel free to reach out to me via e-mail at: michelle@michellekirby.me. Believe in yourself, and help others as a result! You can do it! Now, start…by starting! YOU'VE GOT THIS!

Turn the *Light* Back On

Reference

Jakes, T.D., "Why God Allows the Enemy to Attack You," https://youtu.be/EyBemXVrNbo.

Turn the *Light* Back On

Appendix A

Important Emergency Services

National Suicide Prevention Lifeline

1-800-273-8255 suicidepreventionlifeline.org

Domestic Violence Hotline 1-800-799-7233

thehotline.org

Sleep Deprivation personal research link:

10 surprising facts about sleep deprivation source:

WebMD

https://www.webmd.com/sleep-disorders/features/10-results-sleep-loss

If you feel you need to seek professional help in any area of your life reach out to someone at church, your family and/or if employed, your health care provider's wellness program can better

assist and guide you with programs available.

Appendix B

(Books I read throughout my healing journey)

THE BIBLE

A Mind in Transformation, Dr. Genaro Marin

Healing and Restoring the Heart, Denise Boggs

Intentional Living, John C Maxwell

Managing your emotions, Joyce Meyer

You're Loved No Matter What, Gerth

Pursuit (Success is hidden in the journey), Dexter Yager and John Mason

The 40 Day Soul Fast, Dr. Cindy Trimm

Commanding your morning, Dr. Cindy Trimm

Prevail, Dr. Cindy Trimm

The Prosperous Soul, Dr. Cindy Trimm

The Necessity of the Enemy, Pastor Ron Carpenter

Good to Great, Jim Collins

5 Love Languages, Gary Chapman

Live, Love, Lead, Brain Houston

Becoming the Woman God Wants Me To Be,

Bartow

Chocolate for a Mother's Heart, Kay Allenbaugh

Beautifully Broken, Kimberly Jones Pothier (*Real*

Talk Kim)

The Best Salesman that ever lived, Og Mandino

<u>Daily Devotional Recommendations</u>

Jesus Calling, Sarah Young

Jesus Today, Sarah Young

Starting your day right, Joyce Meyers

New Day New You, Joyce Meyers

Ending your day right, Joyce Meyers

Commanding your morning, Cindy Trimm

Hi God, it's me again, Nicole Crank

Michelle Kirby

Grace for the moment, Day/Eve Edition, Max

Lucado

Turn the *Light* Back On

Michelle Kirby

Appendix C

(Testimony of a nervous breakdown experience/ verbatim interview with a Sister/Friend)

"Michelle, between April 2016 and January 2017 I dealt with a similar situation like you. I noticed that things started happening and shifting downward after I went on a consecration weekend in December of 2016 and then things of my past just started revealing themselves as well as just "life" things becoming overwhelming. This coincidentally happened after I held a women's event in which 60 of them received the baptism of the Holy Spirit and they left completely empowered! I felt isolated, I was physically ill, paralyzed even. I was in denial that I didn't feel well, so I just kept moving. I would read the

Bible, I would speak faith and then 4 days after the women's event I physically could not even stand. My stomach was a mess and internally nothing was functioning well.

I went to the doctor and I remember it was a Tuesday night (went to a MD 360) I remember telling them that I felt like I had a broken rib. They did a bunch of tests, a bunch of diagnostics and nothing! The doctors said "nothing is wrong with her" so on Wednesday I even went to church to lead worship but I was in so much pain I couldn't even stand up! I had to lay down. Thursday I went to my family doctor and explained the occurrences of the past few days and he said "nothing is physically wrong with you, you are having a nervous breakdown and your body needs to shut down. I believe you can do this at home with the support system you have". I chose to go home instead of the behavioral hospital and the doctor sent me away with medication to shut down my body. He urged me of the importance of staying home through this time and said that I was not to leave my house until I was well. Unfortunately, my daughter had a test scheduled at the hospital the next day, and as a mom I couldn't miss it. It was a test on her heart to see if the heart murmur was something that would go away, or if something serious was going on with her heart. My anxiety completely had taken over at this point. We went out to eat lunch right after that appointment and my husband had to carry me because I passed out in the restaurant.

Michelle for 30 days I was out of it. I felt like I had lost my mind. My husband would take me out on drives to calm me. I didn't take care of my kids, I physically couldn't, but my husband was so sweet and so gentle he covered me and I was to have no contact with anyone. He took my

cell phone and handled my affairs during this

time. I had the time to reflect and realized that I

needed healing-BIG TIME. There were things in

my past, teenage things, feelings, religion that had

put serious expectations on my life. I carried them

all as a weight. My strong mentality and my pride

just had to go. I was done being that strong

woman that could handle it all. I have filled my

life and my calendar with things to do, busywork,

it was never enough. What occurred at the

consecration weekend was as if the Lord just

opened me up and everything was exposed. I

remember this one specific time I look back on as

my breaking point. My husband knew that

drawing me a bath would calm me down so he

had a bath drawn for me and played "What a

beautiful name" by Hillsong via surround sound

in the entire house (on repeat). He laid on the

bathroom floor and prayed, wept and pleaded with God. He asked me to sing, he said "open your mouth and say something, sing" and I did not say a thing. I couldn't even speak- I felt as if someone took my vocal cords. He kept doing it and he was very persistent, he said "open your mouth and say something"- and all of a sudden I started singing and we both continued singing and crying in the bathroom and that's when I knew I reached my breaking point. My husband knew that he had to lead me to sing, to worship, to be in the presence of God. He knew that if I opened my mouth and sang worship songs that it would begin my healing. The Lord took him and shifted him spiritually and he then started leading our home in worship and being the spiritual leader in the household. As far as sleep is concerned, Michelle I had no sleep pattern, I didn't sleep- I couldn't! I was suffering from severe insomnia.

Another thing that I will tell you that was scary was my husband telling me (a while after I got out of this) that he thought that I was "gone". He thought he had lost his wife. During that time, he was fearful every single time I turned off the worship music and he would turn it back on. He knew what I needed. He knew that it was being in the presence of God that he could help get me back to reality. Those moments were so scary. I was having nightmares, I was so severely depressed that only at that one moment, when I opened my mouth to sing was when I felt some kind of hope".

During my healing journey, I also came across another friend who also leads worship and we talked and found out that she had a similar situation, but no one knew about it because she also dealt with it in isolation. I encourage anyone that is reading this book to please seek help, don't feel that you are alone, don't feel ashamed, you'll come out stronger as a result. I'm a living testament.

After all this went down the vision came to me to birth my new ministry and ever since then I don't look back. I realized that I have to be a daughter first and then a pastor. I had those things flipped I wanted to be a pastor and then a daughter of the Most High, God. I realized that I had to receive God's love first and then He would walk with me to help me achieve any task. It's as if God was just saying "sit down and rest your mind, His discipline was just a sitting down, not a reprimand or condemnation but He wanted me to just walk with Him".

Your sister in Christ.

xoxo

Since breaking my silence:

- A ministry has been birthed that will impact Nations
- A team has been formed to walk along side of me
- I have so much more compassion and love for those who are hurting
- My priorities are now: God, Husband, Kids, Ministry
- My relationships with everyone around me is much stronger
- Authenticity is no longer an option in my life, but a necessity

Appendix D

(A relevant word by TD Jakes, Why God allowed the enemy to attack you)

"There's a level in God that you can become that you learn through your trials and your tests and your enemies and your frustrations help to teach you who you are in God. If you were not going through what you were going through, you would not know that you are significant. Some of you have not allowed your struggles to work for you. You have got to start reasoning and understanding that the attacks that come against you do not fit where you are.

There is no way that the enemy could afford to invest that much fight into you over where you are. He is not concerned about where you are, he is not intimidated by what you have done. The reason that he has loosed his fortresses against

you is not over what you have done to this point.
The enemy has signed a warrant for your arrest
because he knows what God is about to do IN
YOUR LIFE! And if you begin to understand
that the warfare that you been up against is a
crazy warfare, it's a ridiculous warfare, it's a
warfare that defies human reasoning suddenly you
begin to ask yourself "well WHO AM I, that I
would go through what I'm going through[1]".
Nobody brings bulldozers and trucks and heavy
equipment to build a chicken coop. When you see
heavy equipment pulling up on the property it
means there is going to be massive construction.
By the same token if you're gonna to tear up a
chicken coop, you don't try to, you can come in
and kick it down, but if you're gonna tear down a
skyscraper you have to release explosives and
dynamites and force. Don't you understand that
the attack that God *allowed* the enemy to send

against you is actually meant to tip you off to who you really are, and when you understand it you will say "it is good for me that I have been afflicted[2]", if I haven't been afflicted I would have thought I was insignificant. I didn't understand why you counted me worthy[3] to go through the fight that I'm going through. I MUST BE SOMEBODY. You must have something planned[4] for me, I mean something that eyes have not seen and ears haven't heard[5] and hasn't entered into your heart.

What I'm trying to gracefully tell you is that many times the enemy is more aware of who you are…than you are".

[1] James 1:2 (NIV) Consider it pure joy, my brothers and sisters, whenever you face trials of many kinds.

[2] Psalm 119:71 (NIV) It was good for me to be afflicted so that I might learn your decrees.

[3] 2 Thessalonians 1:11 (NIV) With this in mind, we constantly pray for you, that our God may make you worthy of his calling, and that by his power he may bring to fruition your every desire for goodness and your every deed prompted by faith.

[4] Jeremiah 29:11 (NIV) "For I know the plans I have for you" says the Lord, "plans to prosper you and not to harm you, plans to give you hope and a future".

[5] 1 Corinthians 2:9 (NIV) "What no eye has seen, what no ear has heard, and what no human mind has conceived" the things God has prepared for those who love him.

Michelle Kirby